John Kennedy

BELFAST CELTIC

John Kennedy

John Kennedy was born in Belfast in 1952, the third of a family of eight. A graduate of Queen's University, Belfast, he is Head of Classical Subjects at a grammar school in Ballymena, Northern Ireland, where he has been teaching since 1976. He now lives in that town with his wife and three sons.

Being a native of West Belfast, and having a keen interest in football, he was inevitably brought up on stories of the legendary Belfast Celtic teams of the past. When the bulldozers moved in to flatten Celtic Park in 1983 to make way for a shopping complex, he decided to write a history of the club from the beginning. This book is a direct result of that research.

Bill McKavanagh

Bill McKavanagh, who has written the Foreword, has had a lifelong interest in Belfast Celtic. Like countless thousands of supporters, he learned about the famous club at his father's knee where the bedtime stories recalled the exploits of Mickey Hamill, the Mahood Brothers, Sammy Curran and Jackie McGrillen. His own memories centre around the great teams of the Thirties and Forties when Scott's Invincibles swept all before them.

Some years ago he began collecting old photographs, newspaper reports, documents and memorabilia, with a view to handing on the legacy of his father to future generations. The resulting sound/slide show 'The Belfast Celtic Story' took West Belfast by storm and attracted overflow attendances wherever it was presented, helping to ensure that the 'Grand Old Team' will continue to live in the hearts and minds of football fans everywhere.

BELFAST CELTIC

JOHN KENNEDY

FOREWORD BY BILL McKAVANAGH

Published by Pretani Press

First published 1989 **Pretani Press**
638, Springfield Road, Belfast BT12 7DY

A Nosmada Book
ISBN 0 948868 12 0

Printed by The Universities Press, Belfast.

Contents

Acknowledgements vi

Foreword vii

Introduction ix

Part One - The Start of the Legend 1891 - 1920

I.   The Beginning — 1891-96 3
II. From Junior Team to Senior Champions — 1896-1900 7
III. Good Times, Bad Times — 1900-12 11
IV. The End of the Beginning — 1912-20 21

Part Two - Austin's Team 1924 - 1934

I.   The Glory Days Begin — 1924-28 33
II. Four in a Row — 1928-29 41
III. Years of Transition — 1929-34 47

Part Three - Elisha's Team 1934 - 1949

I.   Scott's Unstoppable Machine — 1934-39 55
II. Five in a Row — 1939-40. 69
III. The Machine Rolls On — 1940-47 73
IV. A Historic Season — 1947-48 85
V. The Jimmy Jones Incident — 1948 -49 91

Epilogue 97

Statistical Appendixes 101

Acknowledgements

I am indebted to Bill McKavanagh for his invaluable support during the production of this history. I am particularly thankful to him for supplying the Foreword and a number of player profiles. Many of the photographs included come also from his excellent slide show on Belfast Celtic, and these were supplied by several people, including John Doris of the Roddy McCorley Social Club, Jimmy McAlinden, Norman Kernaghan, Jimmy Jones, Harry Walker, Harry Vernon, Mrs R.P. Fulton, Mrs T. Breen, Mrs C. Campbell, J.J. Tohill, James Donnelly, Michael McGuigan and John Duffy.

Many thanks are also due to the staff of the Linenhall and Central Libraries for their kind assistance, and to Samuel Adamson of Pretani Press for his advice and guidance.

A special word of thanks to my wife, who patiently typed and retyped the manuscript with hardly a word of complaint!

John Kennedy.

Foreword

Belfast Celtic! There was magic in the name. It whispers of nostalgia and sentiment and pride. The name reaches back across the mists of yesteryear to touch that most bittersweet of emotions, our lost youth, when the world was bright and innocent and heroes walked tall.

Belfast Celtic! They were undeniably the greatest football team this island of Ireland has ever produced, and measured against the teams of today their play was exciting and revolutionary. It is nothing short of amazing that today, forty years after their untimely departure from the game, their memory and their exploits still shine brightly in the hearts and minds of the people of West Belfast.

John Kennedy has produced an extraordinary history of this great club. He takes us from their early beginnings among the working class of the Falls Road, the titanic battles against all who sought a niche in history by defeating them, the stormy periods of political unrest and the records established so long ago that still stand.

Once again, the names come tumbling down the stairs of time. Scott, Hamill, McAlinden, Fulton, O'Connor, Breen, Walker, Kernaghan; there were giants among us and John Kennedy leads us along the path of tears and cheers that still excite us now so long after the curtain has fallen.

And the records! Four League Championships in a row, followed by seven in succession; seven players on one international team; a centre forward who scored eleven goals in one match, which remains a British record to this day; strikers who constantly scored from 70 to 80 goals in a season; the first Irish team to play in Europe, and then the jewel in the crown, the victory over Scotland, holders of the British International championship, in 1949.

Belfast Celtic did not need John Kennedy's book to keep their memory alive. That has already been ensured by their long and glorious history, and from generation to generation in West Belfast the stories and the legends are handed down. Rather, his book is more of a monument to an institution that was more than just a football team. They were a symbol at a time when the people of West Belfast had little else. 'When we had nothing,' it is said, 'we had Belfast Celtic - and then we had everything.'

John Kennedy is to be congratulated on producing what will undoubtedly be the definitive history of this magnificent club. It is splendidly researched, graphically written and scrupulously fair, and certainly belongs not only in the sporting history of the country, but also in its social and cultural background. We will never see their like again, but this book has given us the opportunity to remember with pride the men of the 'Grand Old Team'.

Bill McKavanagh

BELFAST CELTIC FOOTBALL CLUB
U.S.A. TOUR
MAY - JUNE   1949.

BELFAST CELTIC 2 GOALS   SCOTLAND NIL

STANDING: E. SCOTT, DR. McSPARRAN, J. LAWLER, J. DOUGLAS, J. MURDOUGH, M. O'FLANAGAN, W. McMILLAN, K. McALINDEN, C. CURRIE, R. SIMPSON, P. McALINDEN, A. DONNELLY
(MANAGER) (DIRECTOR)   (DIRECTOR) (CHAIRMAN)

P. McGUIGAN, A. MOORE, J. CAMPBELL, G. HAZLETT, J. DENVER, H. WALKER, T. AHERNE, P. BONNAR, T. DORMAN
(TRAINER)   (CAPTAIN)

Introduction

In the summer of 1949, Belfast Celtic Football Club undertook a tour of the U.S.A. and Canada. In the event, it was a 'farewell' tour, as the club had just withdrawn from Irish League Football in tragic circumstances. While in America, Celtic proved to be excellent ambassadors for Belfast and for Ireland. They won six and drew two of their ten matches, and made countless friends along the way. One match goes down in the annals of football as being particularly noteworthy.

On Sunday, May 29th, Celtic played the sixth match of their tour, against the Scottish International side. The venue was the Triborough Stadium, Randall's Island, New York. No-one in the 15,000 crowd expected Celtic to win. The Scots were the current British Champions, having recently disposed of England by three goals to one at Wembley. Their team consisted of such great names as Billy Steel, Willie Waddell and Glasgow Celtic's Bobby Evans, described by the legendary Charlie Tully as the best player he had ever seen.

But the Belfast team played with a glorious disregard for reputations. Although Scotland attacked almost incessantly, they found goalkeeper Kevin McAlinden in literally unbeatable form. Full-backs Billy McMillen and 'Bud' Aherne were no less outstanding. Centre-half Charlie Currie always had the measure of Scottish target-man Thornton. Robin Lawlor was reckoned to be the best half-back on the pitch, while captain Harry Walker played with the commanding consistency that made him one of the most popular Celtic players ever.

With the game almost half-an-hour old, McMillen eased the pressure with a long kick out of defence. The ball reached Tom Dornan. A high cross from the clever inside-right was met by the powerful head of centre-forward Johnny Campbell. Jim Brown in the Scotland goal was like a drowning man clutching at a straw, as he watched the ball sail past him into the net. Celtic were a goal up.

In the second-half, Lawlor took a long throw-in, which landed in the penalty area. Brown came out to claim it, but was unsuccessful. As the ball dropped, Campbell was first to react. The big Derryman drove the ball into the back of the net to score his, and Celtic's second. There was no further scoring, so the game ended with the remarkable result - SCOTLAND 0, BELFAST CELTIC 2.

The Celtic team for this historic win contained three 'guest' players. The full team consisted of: McAlinden; McMillen and Aherne; Walker, Currie and Lawlor; Moore (Glenavon), Dorman (Ards), Campbell, O'Flanaghan (Bohemians) and Bonnar.

The victory over Scotland was the final episode in the 60-year history of the great club from Belfast. This book will follow its progress, from its humble beginnings in 1891, through the crises of the early 1900's, the unprecedented triumphs of the Twenties and Thirties, and the successes of the War years , to the terrible incident that led to its withdrawal from football.

Mayor William O'Dwyer of New York welcomes Belfast Celtic to America

Kevin McAlinden makes a daring save against the British International Champions, Scotland, in New York

PART ONE

The Start of The Legend

1891 - 1920

Belfast Celtic circa 1893

I

The Beginning — 1891-1896

THE story of Belfast Celtic begins in the city's Falls Park - with a game of cricket! On a fine Saturday evening in August 1891, a team called the 'Sentinel', which claimed to be the willow-wielding champions of the Falls, played a challenge match against the celebrated 'Model Star'. This latter team brought a great reputation with them. It consisted of many experienced and well-travelled cricketers, who circulated stories of having played 'on the sun-baked pitches of Africa and in the heat of an Indian summer'. However, these globe-trotters turned out to be no match for the 'Sentinel' team, who ended up by giving their opponents a convincing thrashing.

After the match, the elated members of the victorious team concluded that the Falls area contained an untapped mine of sporting talent, which was just waiting to be exploited. Two of the players, Bob Haynes and Frank Laverty, were well-known in football circles, having played for Milltown, another Junior team from the area. Along with Alex Begley and James Keenan, they formed the opinion that there would be enough interest in and around the Falls to form a decent football club, which would rival or even surpass the team from Milltown. With this in mind, they held a meeting in the rooms of Mr James Henry on the Falls Road. At this historic meeting, it was decided to call the new club Belfast Celtic, after their famous Glasgow namesakes.

Belfast Celtic's close fraternal association with the Glasgow club, which was to last throughout its history, was initiated at this first meeting. One of secretary Bob Hayes' first duties was to write to Glasgow Celtic asking for their patronage. Not only did they consent to grant it, but they also sent a generous and welcome donation to help the new Celtic to become established.

The club's first officers were: President, James McCann; Honorary Secretary, Bob Hayes; Match Secretary, Alex Begley; Treasurer, James Keenan; Captain, Frank Laverty. These were the men who originated the finest football club that Ireland has ever seen.

Celtic's first ground was secured at Broadway, just below the Beehive public house. Because of the less than ideal underfoot condition of the pitch, and the general lack of grass, the 'stadium' was soon given the unflattering nickname of 'Boghead' - a variation, of course, on 'Parkhead', the home of Glasgow Celtic.

After obtaining the pitch, the next logical step was to play some football on it. An invitation to a challenge match was duly extended to Glentoran II, one of the best Junior teams in the city. Although Celtic were beaten in this, their first ever match, the supporters of the new team were suitably impressed by their performance. After all, most of the team had as yet no experience of top-class football, and there was a firm belief that there were great days ahead.

In that same first season, Celtic decided to enter the Junior Cup and County Antrim Shield, but were beaten in the first rounds of both competitions. This was perhaps one of the most crucial periods in the club's entire history. Because of their lack of early success, there were those who believed that the team was destined not to make the grade, and should therefore be disbanded. Thankfully, there was no such air of pessimism among the majority of the players. They continued to play at Broadway, and during the season were admitted into the Junior Alliance.

Before the end of the season, Celtic were well-established in Junior football. The team's ever-growing reputation was enhanced by two notable victories. The first was a 9-2 thrashing of top Junior League team Linfield Swifts, the second was a popular 3-2 away win over local rivals Milltown.

In the second year of their existence, Celtic were admitted to the Junior League. They immediately made their presence felt by finishing runners-up to Distillery II. Then began a period of total Celtic domination of the Junior ranks. For the next three seasons, they were almost unbeatable as they chalked up a hat-trick of Junior League Championships. They also won the new and imposing Robinson and Cleaver Shield in the first three years of that competition's existence.

In the 50 league games played during these seasons, Celtic lost a grand total of two. In the 1894/5 season, they actually remained undefeated in the league, obtaining 33 points out of a possible 36.

It was during their short reign as juniors that Celtic won their first senior trophy, the County Antrim Shield in 1895. They had reached the final of the same competition in the previous two seasons, only to be beaten 2-1 on both occasions by Distillery and Cliftonville. However, 1895 proved to be a case of third time lucky.

Distillery were again the opponents in the final at Cliftonville's ground, Solitude. The senior team were the obvious favourites, but at the end of the ninety minutes Celtic were the worthy holders of the trophy, winning by three goals to one. Centre-forward Pat McAuley was the hero, as indeed he was to be five years later when his club won the Irish league for the first time in their history. He scored Celtic's first two goals, while centre-half Pat Farrell got the third.

·BELFAST·CELTIC·FOOTBALL·TEAM·
Winners of "Robinson & Cleaver Shield" 1894 & 95.

It was fitting that Farrell, the team captain, should get his name on the score-sheet, as he had been the pivot around which this great team turned. He was one of the strongest players of the Nineties, as was his left-wing partner Jack McConville, who was to take over the captainship on Pat's departure.

It is worth recording the full Celtic line-up for this historic win: Blakeley; Strannigan and Lavery; McKeown, Farrell and McConville; McGarry, Stilges, McAuley, Kelly and Breen.

Just one month after their Antrim Shield success, Celtic challenged Linfield to a 'friendly' match at Broadway. Although reports of the match are somewhat uncertain, it can be ascertained that Celtic won 5-1 after being a goal down at half-time, and that three of the winning goals came from Farrell, McAuley and outside-left Jim Kelly.

The Celtic team that day contained the exciting right-wing partnership of Pat McGarry and Charlie Breen. Some 30 years later, Mr. Joe Ferguson, an IFA official and one of the most respected figures in football at the time, declared in 'The Celt'[1] that the McGarry/Breen right-wing was the best he had ever seen in Irish Football. Great praise indeed from a man who had seen many great players.

Celtic's last match as a junior team came on 30 May 1896. Linfield Swifts, their main rivals for junior honours, provided the opposition in the Junior Charity Shield Final. Goals from McConville and McAuley turned a one-goal half-time deficit into a 2-1 win at the final whistle. Celtic therefore ended their spell in the junior ranks with another victory and another trophy.

1. 'The Celt' was the name of Belfast Celtic's official programme.

II

From Junior Team to Senior Champions — 1896-1900

Because of their singular successes and obvious superiority as juniors, the IFA promoted Celtic to senior football for the 1896/97 season. The club's officials were opposed to the promotion. The Broadway pitch, never in great condition at the best of times, had become totally unplayable the previous season, and they had found themselves without a home ground. They preferred to wait until such times as they obtained a stadium of their own before taking such an important step. However, their objections fell upon deaf ears, and along with the North Staffordshire regiment, Celtic joined the four established clubs Distillery, Glentoran, Cliftonville and Linfield in a six-team league.

During this, their first season in the Irish League, the Celtic team found the gap between junior and senior football too wide, and the lack of a pitch of their own too big a disadvantage. For the first and last time in history, a Belfast Celtic team finished last in the league. Hardly an auspicious start to senior football. At least there was one consolation in this dismal season - things could only get better!

The following season, 1897/98, things did begin to take a turn for the better. The change in fortunes came when, with the league almost over, Celtic moved into their own grounds. 13 November 1897 was the memorable date when Celtic Park, adjacent to the City Cemetery on the Falls/Whiterock Road, was opened.

About the same time in far-off Canada, another event was in progress which had caught the imagination of the world. Gold had been discovered at a small river in the Yukon Territory, and hopeful prospectors were converging there from all corners of the globe. The name of the river was Klondyke, and this was the nickname that was soon given to the new Celtic Park by the supporters. No doubt they were eagerly anticipating a 'goal' rush of their own!

The first guests at the new enclosure were the King's Own Regiment in the first round of the Irish Cup. The supporters who flocked to 'Klondyke' were treated to a 5-1 victory for Celtic. The following Saturday the team played host to Distillery, who were beaten by the same margin. The patient Celtic fans had something to cheer about at last. From the opening of the Klondyke in November until the end of the season in May, they remained unbeaten in home matches. As a result, they finished the City Cup competition as runners-up to Linfield.

In 1898/9, Celtic had their best Cup run to date. In the first round they were in magnificent form against Cliftonville, scoring seven goals without reply. After disposing of St. Columb's Court, Derry, in the second round, they met Glentoran in the semi-final.

The semi-final illustrates an interesting but unwelcome aspect of football in this period. Scarcely a week went by without the IFA's Senior Protests and Appeals Committee being called upon to make a judgement on some dispute arising out of the previous Saturday's matches. The losing team would protest at the state of the pitch, the ineligibility of a player on the opposing team, the height, width or lack of goal posts, the match kicking off a couple of minutes before or after the stipulated time, or anything else that might obtain a replay.

After a draw in the first semi-final, Glentoran won the replay 2-1. Celtic lodged a successful protest on the grounds that the Glens were fielding an ineligible player, and a second replay was needed. Celtic won 2-1, but this time Glentoran lodged an objection on the same grounds. When this protest was also upheld, the tie went to a fourth match.

What should have been a classic encounter between two finely balanced sides was ruined by a crowd of hooligans. With Glentoran two up in the second half, these so-called 'supporters' invaded the pitch and engaged in a disgraceful bout of fighting. The referee had no option but to abandon the match. As Glentoran had been winning at the time, the Appeals Committee awarded them the match.

Sadly, the hooliganism which accompanied this match was nothing new. In fact, it was in evidence in Celtic's very first season in senior football. In only the second game of that season, police had to come between fighting factions at the Glentoran-Celtic match. There was also trouble at a Celtic-Linfield game, with Celtic's Terry Devlin being attacked by a handful of Linfield 'supporters'. A similar, more serious incident over fifty years later was to lead to the permanent withdrawal of Belfast Celtic from football.

Incidents among rival fans in the 1899/1900 season resulted in the police erecting posters at all the league grounds. These warned the spectators to behave, and threatened them with arrest and prosecution if they failed to do so. Who said that spectator violence was a modern phenomenon?

Crowd trouble apart, this was an extremely satisfying and historic season for Belfast Celtic F.C. During the close season the club's officials, including President Hugh Fitzpatrick and Vice-President Hugh McAlinden, had been busy putting together a well-balanced team. Two of the club's stalwart defenders, full-back George Fleming and captain Jack McConville, had been the target for several cross-channel clubs, but were induced to stay at Celtic Park. Centre-forward Pat McAuley, the first Celtic player to win an Irish International cap,

Hugh McAlinden, Chairman

Robert Barr, Secretary

was as sharp and enthusiastic as ever. Astute signings were also made in centre-half Jimmie Connor from Downpatrick, and Abrahams, an outside-right from Partick Thistle.

The North Staffordshire regiment had withdrawn from the league, and their place was taken by another army team, the Royal Scots. However, there are some things in this world which are more important than football. On the outbreak of the Boer War in mid-season, the Scottish soldiers were sent to South Africa, and the league reverted to just five teams.

During the season, the efforts of the Celtic officials and players were amply rewarded. A goal-less draw with Cliftonville, followed by successive wins over Glentoran and Linfield, set them on the road to their first-ever league title. When the eight-match programme was completed, Celtic emerged as champions for the first time in their history. Pat McAuley was the undoubted star of the team, finding the net eight times in seven matches.

He was ably supported by Harry Dornan, the scorer of four goals, and by Abrahams, Joe Dorrian and Jim Kelly, who each scored a couple. Other players during this historic Championship-winning season included Doran, Tully, Nicholl, McGarry, Anderson, Mitchell, Davidson and popular goalkeeper Frank Magennis.

In this same eventful season, Celtic played a friendly match against a team of 'colourful' South African tourists who rejoiced in the name of the Kaffirs. The exuberant, happy-go-lucky style of the Africans in their bright orange strip was enjoyed by the bumper crowd, who saw Celtic emerge as 5-3 winners.

Belfast Celtic, 1900

III

Good Times, Bad Times — 1900-1912

In 1901 it seemed as if Belfast Celtic were destined to win their first Irish Cup after a 2-0 semi-final victory over Cliftonville. However, the Solitude team lodged an objection to this result on the inaccuracy of the measurements of the goal posts. The protest was successful, Cliftonville won the replay, and went on to beat a Dublin team called Freebooters in the final.

In this season the left-wing partnership of R. Clarke and I. Doherty were honoured with International caps.

The big talking point of the 1901/2 season was the opening of Celtic's fine new stadium. The old Celtic Park had become an eyesore, so the fans deserted the 'Klondyke' for 'Paradise'. Seven acres of land between the Donegall Road and Broadway had been obtained by the far-sighted Celtic directors, who raised the £3,000 needed for the purchase by offering 3,000 shares at £1 each to the public. The little club that had started life just a decade earlier was now called by the grand title of BELFAST CELTIC FOOTBALL AND ATHLETIC COMPANY LIMITED. No expense was spared over the years to make the stadium one of the very best in the British Isles. It was to be the club's permanent home for the remainder of their time in football. (It would be nice to record that Celtic won their first match in Paradise, but the party was spoilt by Glentoran, who beat the home team 3-1.)

At the end of the following season, left-back Billy Clay was transferred to Sheffield United. This was the first in a long series of transfers from Celtic to cross-channel clubs.

In 1904 Celtic won the Belfast Charity Cup, an end-of-season competition whose proceeds went to the Belfast hospitals. They beat Glentoran 1-0 in the final, with the winning goal scored by inside-left Soye. That same season left-half Harry Nicholl gained his first international cap against Wales.

The 1904/5 league competition saw Celtic and Glentoran in an exciting neck-and-neck race for the title. The crucial match between the teams took place on Boxing Day at Celtic Park. Both teams started the match with 14 points from 10 games. By the end, they were still locked together at the top of the table, as the result was a 1-1 draw. They could still not be separated when all the league fixtures were completed, as both teams won their last three matches. In the test match to decide on the outright champions, Glentoran won by three goals to one. Celtic therefore finished in second place.

The hard work of the previous couple of seasons by the players and directors, and the patience of the supporters, was handsomely rewarded in 1905/6. This was the club's first year in the Irish Cup Final. Having beaten Bohemians in the semi-final, Celtic's opponents in the final were another Dublin team, Shelbourne.

Celtic had hoped that the big match would be played at Glentoran's ground, the Oval. However, their hopes were dashed when the IFA Fixtures Committee ruled that the game be played in Dublin. It was virtually a home game for Shelbourne. The Celtic players did not travel well, and the match resulted in a 2-0 win for the Dubliners.

But the disappointment at not winning the Cup was forgotten just a fortnight later, when the City Cup ended up in the boardroom at Celtic Park. It had been an extremely exciting and close-fought competition. After nine matches of the ten-match programme, Celtic and Linfield were equal top, followed by Cliftonville one point behind.

On Easter Monday, the two top teams met at Celtic Park in what should have been the decider. The result, however, was a goal-less draw. As Cliftonville had won their last match, all three teams finished with the same number of points.

A series of test matches was necessary to find the outright winners. Just a week after the Cup Final, Celtic met Linfield in the first of these matches at Grosvenor Park. Putting all memories of Dublin behind them, Celtic completely outclassed the Blues, winning 2-0. The following Saturday's match against Cliftonville was to be the final decider. This time Celtic made no mistake. A 2-0 victory gave them their first-ever City Cup.

Celtic retained the same trophy the following season, this time without having to resort to a test match. At the end of the campaign they had registered six wins and three draws out of ten matches. In retaining the cup, they scored a very commendable 23 goals.

Celtic's team over these seasons generally consisted of Haddock; Watson and McCartney; McCann, Connor and Pinkerton; Gall, Mulholland, Gillespie, Maxwell and Devlin. Both inside forwards, Steve Mulholland and Jim Maxwell, had their consistency rewarded by being picked to play for the Irish international team. Alex McCartney and Jimmy Connor were also capped for Ireland.

The next few seasons were more noteworthy for what happened off the field than on it. Indeed, this was a period of dramatic crises for the club - crises which almost culminated in its withdrawal from football.

12

Celtic Park - 'Paradise' - looking over at the Unreserved Stand

The first crisis came in the 1907/8 season. The Celtic Directors were irate at the IFA's continual refusal to allow Celtic Park to be used as a venue for internationals or important cup matches. This was in spite of the fact that the directors had gone to great lengths to make Paradise one of the best enclosures in Ireland. The board actually made up their minds to leave, and only decided to continue when asked to do so by the club's most prominent and influential supporters.

The second crisis came the following season, with the introduction of the notorious 'Rough Play' Commission. This body took it upon itself to suspend Celtic and Cliftonville from football because of incidents arising out of a Charity Cup match. The two clubs retorted by sending letters of withdrawal to the IFA. The ruling body realised that the withdrawal of two of the league's most prestigious teams would be financially disastrous. Not surprisingly, they were very quick to withdraw the suspensions. Celtic and Cliftonville in turn consented to return to league football.

The third and most serious crisis came in the 1909/10 season. Again it centred around the treatment of Celtic by the gentlemen of the IFA Council. The trouble arose out of a cup match against Bohemians at Celtic Park. During the game, the Celtic centre-forward Neal Clarke was sent off for kicking the Bohemians' left-back. This prompted a section of the crowd to rush onto the pitch and mob the referee, who retreated to the pavilion.

The incident was referred to the Protest and Appeals Committee. There was no question that Clarke was guilty of kicking, and that he should be duly punished. But it was the nature of the punishment that shocked and dismayed the Celtic connections. It was decided to suspend the player until January 1911 - a massive ten-month sentence. Yet players from other clubs who had been found guilty of similar offences were only given a one-month suspension.

To further aggravate the situation, it was decided at the same meeting to close Celtic Park for one month. This was another totally unexpected and unprecedented blow. Although their supporters had acted deplorably, they had not acted any differently than those of other clubs. Yet these clubs had not had their grounds closed.

This was the last straw for the Celtic directors. Their conviction that they were being victimised by the IFA was now apparent to all. They unanimously decided to abandon Association Football, and this time had the full backing of their shareholders. On hearing the decision, the IFA Council met to reconsider the 'sentence'. No doubt realising the importance of Celtic's contribution to their revenue, they had no option but to rescind the sentence on Clarke, deeming it to be harsh and unjustified. In light of this decision, the directors reversed their decision to withdraw.

Despite all their trials and tribulations, the 1909/10 season proved to be a very satisfying one for Celtic in terms of results. This was in spite of the fact that three of their star players had been transferred to Sheffield Wednesday at the end of the previous season. These were right-back P. Warren, centre-forward P. O'Connell, and captain Andy Hunter, an international outside-right.

Celtic won two trophies late in the season. The first of these was the County Antrim Shield, which they had last won in the days when they were still juniors. The final against Glentoran took place at Solitude. Andy Davidson was the Celtic marksman, scoring two goals in the last eleven minutes to effectively end the Glens' challenge. Willie Briggs added a third to give Celtic a 3-1 win.

Left-back Pat McCann won his first cap in the same season. Celtic's inside-right in the Antrim Shield victory was a young local man who was to have a profound effect on the history of Belfast Celtic for more than twenty years - the great Mickey Hamill. Many people would argue that Mickey was the greatest player ever to wear the green-and-white jersey. They could well be right.

Mickey's transfer to Manchester United, then the leaders of the English First Division, was the main talking point of the following season. The Falls Road man's popularity with the Celtic fans was well-illustrated on his departure for Manchester. No less than 2,000 fans turned up at the station to see him off. Happily the transfer was not the end of Hamill's association with the Belfast club; he was to return some three years later among even greater scenes of adulation.

The second trophy destined for Celtic's sideboard in 1910 was the Charity Cup. Celtic met Distillery in the final. The match ended in a 2-2 draw, with Briggs and Charlie Crothers the Celtic marksmen. The replay was decided by 2 goals from Antrim Shield hero Andy Davidson, as Celtic emerged 2-1 winners.

A feature of the 1911/12 season was the introduction of Lurgan team Glenavon to league football, Bohemians having withdrawn. Celtic's first match in Lurgan was accompanied by a truly carnival atmosphere. Special trains were laid on to take the Celtic supporters - 1,500 of them - to the match. This was the real beginning of the 'football excursions'. For the ordinary Celtic supporter, Dublin and Derry were too far away, and therefore too expensive to travel to. However, they could get to Lurgan and back for a shilling.

The sight of 1,500 Celtic fans marching through the streets of Lurgan was a new one to that town's inhabitants, who had eagerly anticipated the match. The local sports shop owner proudly displayed the match ball in his shop window,

Mickey Hamill

Many great footballers played for Belfast Celtic during the club's 60-year history. Mickey Hamill, born and reared on the City's Falls Road, was one of the greatest. From his first appearance in the team in 1909, until the time he picked up his fifth League Championship medal some 20 years later, Mickey was idolised by the Celtic faithful.

Always an inspiration to his team-mates, he is remembered for having captained Ireland to their first-ever Home Championship win in 1914. That same year, he returned to Celtic Park after a few seasons with Manchester United. He proceeded to lead Celtic - sporting their new strip of green and white hoops - to their first league Championship in 15 years.

In 1918 Mickey was the inspiration behind Belfast Celtic's first-ever Cup victory, a 2-0 win over arch-rivals Linfield. He helped them to another league win in 1920.

During Celtic's enforced absence from football in the early Twenties, Mickey again moved across the water. He had spells with Manchester City and Glasgow Celtic, before emigrating to Boston, Massachusetts, where he played for the Forth River team.

At the age of 37, when most players' footballing days are fast becoming a distant memory, Mickey was about to embark upon the most successful phase of his career. In the 1926/27 season he returned to Belfast, and was immediately promoted into Elisha Scott's all-conquering team. He was an integral part of that team for the next 3 seasons, picking up a hat-trick of Championship medals before hanging up his boots at 40.

A true folk-hero of his native Falls Road, Mickey Hamill was the first of football's superstars.

along with an exhortation to the people of Lurgan to go and support the home team. The match ended in a 2-0 win for the visitors, and 1,500 Belfast men went home happy.

The same season was fraught with friction between the clubs and the IFA over gate money in cup matches. The friction culminated in all the senior clubs except Linfield breaking away from the IFA and forming their own association. A 'New Irish Cup' competition, which became known as the Gold Cup, was instituted. Celtic reached the final of the competition in its first year, when they met Glentoran.

In this match, Celtic played what many of their long-standing supporters reckoned to be their best game. Oscar Traynor in goals had an immaculate game. The defence, with centre-half Jimmy Connor dominating as ever, was unflinching. The team play of the forwards baffled the Glentoran defence. In fact, the forward line of Louis Crowe, Jordan Robertson, Sam Hill, Billy Marshall and Harry Buckle was one of Celtic's finest. A combination of Robertson, Crowe and Buckle resulted in the latter scoring a neat first-half goal. In the second half, Robertson put the icing on the cake when he drove a 30-yard shot into the top corner of the net. The final result was a 2-0 win for Celtic. Other Celtic players in this historic win were Willie Laverty, Jimmy Nelson, Sam Palmer and Tom Lewis.

Also in 1911/12, Celtic won the Charity Cup for the second time in three years. Ten thousand people turned up on a fine May afternoon to watch the final against Distillery. As in the Gold Cup Final, the passing play of the forwards provided a major headache for the opposition's defence. Norwood and Grant were playing in place of Hill and Marshall, and fully justified their selection when they scored a goal each. Bob Norwood was also responsible for setting up a third goal for Buckle. The result was a convincing 3-1 win for Celtic.

The Charity Cup Final was in effect a farewell performance by the Celtic team, for the following Saturday they set out on a history-making tour of Czechoslovakia, or 'Gay Bohemia' as it was then called. Three weeks later the players returned from the tour with an abundance of tales, tall or otherwise.

After a couple of victories over the Slavian sporting club of Prague, the tourists travelled to Pardubice on the River Elbe. They were totally unprepared for the onslaught of 'eleven live-wire Bohemian gentlemen', whose lack of skill was more than compensated for by sheer enthusiasm and determination. The goalkeeper had all the credentials for the Tarzan role - he was six feet four, weighed sixteen stone at a conservative guess, and could fist the ball from his own penalty area into that of the opposition. Then there was the prolific inside-left by the name of Kojak, who was reputed to have scored 800 goals in just 5 seasons.

The frisky Bohemian forwards were buzzing around so busily that at one stage Jimmy Nelson sat on top of one after he had fallen. When asked to give a reason for his action, Jimmy declared that it was quite an effective way of knocking off a yard or two in pace. The result, a 3-1 win for the home team, was the only defeat for Celtic on the 6-match tour.

It seems, however, that football was only an incidental part of the tour. It was the first time that most of the party had been abroad, and they obviously revelled in experiencing the Continental way of life. They recalled with amusement the donkey sausages, and the tea that was 'milked' with cognac. Club Director Hugh McAlinden - obviously a seasoned traveller - had the foresight to bring several packets of tea with him on the trip. Needless to say, Hugh soon became the most popular member of the party.

Then there was the story of Jimmy Connor, who was approached by a waiter in the House of Representatives in Prague. Instead of taking Jimmy's order, as expected, the waiter asked him how all the folk in Downpatrick were getting along. It transpired that the waiter had worked in the Slieve Donard Hotel in Newcastle, and had recognised the Celtic centre-half as soon as he came in. It was a small world even in those pre-Concorde days.

This first-ever tour of Europe by an Irish side was a singular success. A good time was had by all, and they even got around to playing a bit of football.

Oscar Traynor

Oscar Traynor, Belfast Celtic's goalkeeper in the 1912 Gold Cup-winning team and on the European Tour, was to become one of the best-known and most highly-respected figures in Irish politics. Born in Dublin into a strongly nationalist family, Oscar took part in the Easter Week Rising in 1916.

He was later an important figure in the War of Independence, and led the Dublin Brigade's attack on the Customs House in 1921.

In 1925, he was elected TD for Dublin North. The ex-goalkeeper held the post of Minister of Defence in several Fianna Fail governments, until his resignation in 1961 due to ill-health.

Throughout his political career, Oscar retained his great love for the game of football. In 1948, he was appointed President of the FAI, a post he held until his death in 1963.

Belfast Celtic, 1911/12
Back Row (left to right): C. Murphy, R. Barr (Secretary), E. Magee, D. McCloskey, P. Dobbin.
Middle Row: J. McIlvenney (Trainer), W. Anderson, G. McGivern, L. Murphy, A. Davidson, G. McClure,
W. Moore, J. Connor.
Front Row: J. McAnerney (IFA), N. Clarke, P. McCann, M. Hamill, C. Crothers (Captain), W. Briggs,
J. Davidson, T. McCann (IFA).

BELFAST CELTIC FOOTBALL CLUB.
THE FIRST IRISH TEAM TO TOUR THE CONTINENT,
(PRAGUE, BOHEMIA, 1912)

BACK ROW: DR DUBROUEN J McANERNEY J CONNOR O TRAYNOR H BUCKLE D BRADY E McALINDEN MRS DR DUBROUEN R BARR
MIDDLE ROW G GIBSON C O'BYRNE L CROWE
FRONT ROW D McCLOSKEY J ROBINSON W MARSHALL W LAVERY R NORWOOD D McCANN J GRANT J NELSON T LEWIS F SMITH H McALINDEN

IV

The End of the Beginning — 1912-1920

1912 was a turbulent year in Belfast. The British government put forward a Home Rule Bill for Ireland. As expected, the Bill was passed in the Liberal-dominated House of Commons, and was due to become law within 2 years.

But the Ulster Unionists would have nothing to do with Home Rule. Their leader, Sir Edward Carson, made it clear that his followers would fight to the death to prevent Home Rule in Ulster.

It was against this tense political background that the 1912/13 football season began. And it was inevitable that the tension should be felt on the terraces, especially when Celtic and Linfield were in opposition.

The first match between the two, at Celtic Park, had to be abandoned at half-time due to a full-scale battle among rival supporters. To the credit of the Linfield directors, they made no claim to the points, to which they were rightfully entitled. Although there were no major disturbances at the replay, it was a very different story when the teams met in November. As the Celtic team took to the field they were greeted by a salvo of gunfire among the home supporters. The firing continued throughout the match, and by the end it was reported that the smell of gunpowder wafted around the ground.

Both teams had the ball in the net 4 times. The referee - showing a remarkable regard for self-preservation - disallowed all 4 Celtic goals, while he let those of Linfield stand. He later claimed in his match report that there was 'nothing unusual about the fans' behaviour'.

The Celtic directors were furious, of course. They lodged a strong protest, and demanded a replay at a neutral venue. But on reflection they decided that, in the best interests of the game, they would withdraw their protest. There were no further serious incidents that season. However, the signs were ominous. Surely it was only a matter of time before something tragic would happen at a Celtic-Linfield match.

For much of the season in which the above scenes took place, and for most of the next one, success eluded Celtic. It was obvious that new blood had to be injected into the club. A new manager, Jimmy Magowan, was appointed at the beginning of the 1914/15 season to bring success back to Celtic Park. New players were drafted in to strengthen the team, among them half-back Sam Ritchie and forward Jack Cowell, a former Distillery player.

The arrival of a new manager and players was totally eclipsed by the sensational return to the club of one of its favourite sons - the great Mickey Hamill. Since his transfer to Manchester United just a few years earlier, Mickey had been widely recognised as one of the best half-backs in the English League. He also had the honour of being the current captain of the Irish side, which had won the Home Championships in the previous season for the first time ever.

The new signings had an immediate impact. For the first match of the season against Bohemians, Mickey Hamill led out his team for the first time in the famous green-and-white hoops - up to this season vertical stripes had been worn. Mickey had an outstanding match at centre-half, as Celtic drew 2-2 with Bohemians. Inside-right Jimmy McKnight scored both goals on his debut.

For the next two months Celtic remained undefeated. The most outstanding forward of the season was Dave Williams, who played either as centre-forward or inside-left. He scored a magnificent hat-trick in a 3-1 win against Cliftonville. The players from Solitude must have thought that Dave had a personal grudge against them, for in the second league encounter between the two teams he put five past their unfortunate goalkeeper. A week later Dave scored twice against Glenavon and the following week in Dublin he scored the only goal of the match against Shelbourne.

By the end of the league programme, Celtic emerged as worthy champions for the second time in their history. Of the fourteen games, they won ten and drew three. In the process, they scored twenty-four goals and conceded only seven. Their fine defensive record was due in no small measure to the outstanding goal-keeping of Bertie Mehaffey who was beaten only three times in the eleven matches he played. Bertie had replaced Fred McKee, a flamboyant character who had endeared himself to the Celtic supporters by his antics on the field. Like Mickey Hamill, Fred was a member of Ireland's Home Championship-winning side. During the close-season he had signed for Linfield.

Jimmy Nelson and Fred Barrett had occupied the full-back positions in all 14 league games, and had come to the rescue of their team mates on numerous occasions. Albert Leathem, who like Barrett had started the season as an untried amateur, played with great composure in the half-back under the steadying influence of Hamill. Bob Norwood and Sam Ritchie shared the left-half position.

While Williams was undoubtedly the star striker, he was ably assisted by Jimmy McKnight and Jack Cowell. Later in the season Jack Hegan and Willie Marshall also played their part in the forward line. Other members of this league-winning team were King, Holt, McKeown, Kerr, Connell and Burns.

Celtic reached the final of the Cup in the same year, only to be beaten 1-0 by

Linfield in a poor match. The Linfield goal was a controversial one, coming as it did after Bertie Mehaffey had been charged by a Linfield forward while not in possession of the ball. Out of the six cup finals between these two great rivals, this was the Blues' only success.

This was, of course, the season which saw the start of the 'Great War'. Although there were calls for a halt to be made for the duration of the war, all the competitions were played as usual. However, it was inevitable that, as the war progressed, the game of football should be disrupted, like so many other activities of everyday life.

In the summer of 1915 the Irish League was put into cold storage for as long as the war lasted. A new Belfast and District League was inaugurated in its place. However, since the members of this league agreed to pay their players a wage, Celtic refused to join. The directors had insisted that all players should revert to amateur status during the war, and would play no part in a professional set-up.

The new competition therefore started under the handicap of the absence of one of its most popular clubs. A new club, Belfast United, took the place of Celtic.

For the next three seasons, Celtic entered a team under the name of Belfast Celtic II in the Intermediate League, with Austin Donnelly as manager. Not surprisingly, with players of Hamill and Barrett's calibre still playing for Celtic, they encountered little opposition.

In 1916/17 the 'Seconds' picked up a trio of Junior trophies: the Intermediate League, the Steel and Sons Cup, and the McIlroy Cup. The team's success was aided by a player who was to become a living legend in Irish football. Elisha Scott was, even at this early stage in his career, the best goalkeeper in Ireland. Even taking the exploits of the great Harry Gregg and Pat Jennings into consideration, there are those who maintain that Elisha was the greatest goalkeeper Ireland ever produced.

In this first season with Celtic, Elisha played an important part in his team's great run in the Irish Cup, even though they were still in junior football.

On the way to the final, they had a fine 2-0 victory over Linfield. 21,000 people turned up at Windsor Park to witness the final between Celtic and Glentoran. Unfortunately, the young Celtic players were unnerved by the occasion. They could not settle down to their normal game, and by the final whistle were a well-beaten side, going down 2-0.

The 1917/18 season saw Celtic still contesting the Intermediate League.

Elisha Scott

Legendary. This is a term often ascribed to Elisha Scott, and deservedly so. For Elisha was indeed a football legend, both as a player and a manager.

As a goalkeeper, he had no peers. Whe he joined Celtic in 1916, he was already recognised as the best in the country. And he was still picking up international caps 20 years later.

Elisha spent most of his playing career on Merseyside, where he became an idol of the Liverpool Kop. His many duels with Everton's Dixie Dean are part of the City's folklore. Scott was the biggest name in the team which won the English League in 1922 and 1923. His total of 429 matches remained a Liverpool record until overtaken in 1958 by Scottish International Billy Liddell.

As a manager, Elisha was equally in a class of his own. Indeed, he can still be regarded as the most successful manager ever in the history of Irish football. This statement is based, not on opinion, but on fact. The statistics say that, under Elisha, Belfast Celtic won 31 major trophies:

Scott's Record

Competition	Years Won	Total
Irish League	*1936, 1937, 1938, 1939, 1940, 1948*	*6*
Irish Cup	*1937, 1938, 1941, 1943, 1944, 1947*	*6*
City Cup	*1940, 1948, 1949*	*3*
Gold Cup	*1935, 1939, 1940, 1941, 1944, 1946, 1947, 1948*	*8*
County Antrim Shield	*1936, 1937, 1939, 1943, 1945*	*5*
Regional League	*1941, 1942, 1947*	*3*

24

Their superiority over the other teams was nothing short of ridiculous. They were scoring about half-a-dozen goals a game, and by the end of the season had dropped only one point. The other teams in the league began to object to the presence of a team that was just too good. However, their objections were somewhat half-hearted; after all, Celtic were drawing the crowds to their grounds, providing them with much-needed revenue during a time of severe financial hardship.

Three times Celtic had contested the Irish Cup Final, and three times they had suffered defeats. Was this the year when that trend was to be reversed? There was certainly an air of optimism in the Celtic camp by the time the first round. was due to be played in February. By this stage they had still to taste defeat, having won the Steel and Sons Cup and collected 18 points from their first 9 league games.

Celtic's first-round opponents were Glentoran. When the match at Celtic Park finished in a goal-less draw, it seemed that the team's involvement in this year's competition would be short-lived. However the replay at the Oval a week later had the sports writers reaching for the superlatives. Against all the odds, the Celtic team emerged as worthy winners, 1-0. The all-important goal was scored by Danny McKinney, a talented outside-right from the Falls Road. In the second round Celtic disposed of Glentoran II, again after a replay. In a hard-fought semi-final against Belfast United, the young Celtic team got through by the odd goal in three. The winning goal was scored by Jimmy Ferris, who was to play a central role in the dominant Celtic team of the Twenties.

The final against Linfield at the Oval ended in a scoreless draw. The stalemate was still unbroken in the replay a fortnight later, when the main talking point was the steep rise in admission prices.

Exorbitant prices or not, a large crowd turned up at Grosvenor Park on an April afternoon to see the second replay. It was a great day in the history of Belfast Celtic Football Club. The eleven Celtic players displayed immense courage and determination and no little skill, in beating the favourites by two goals to nil.

While it was a superb team performance, with Mickey Hamill particularly majestic in defence, the special laurels were reserved for Norman Stewart. The first goal came when he lobbed a free-kick into the Linfield penalty area. One of the opposition's backs miskicked his clearance, and the ball ended up in the back of the net. The second goal was one of the greatest in an Irish Cup Final. Norman obtained the ball in mid-field and made a beeline for Fred McKee in the Linfield goal, beating several opponents en route. He finished perfectly by putting a beautifully-placed shot out of Fred's reach.

The Celtic supporters erupted, scenting victory at last in the Cup. They sang and cheered until the final whistle. Despite valiant efforts by the Linfield forwards to get back on terms, the gritty Celtic defence held out. After eight hard-fought matches and twelve hours of cup football, Celtic won the trophy. Celtic's historic Cup-winning team consisted of Scott; McStay and Barrett; Mulligan, Hamill and Stewart; McKinney, McIlroy, Ferris, Johnston and Frazer.

With the war ending in 1918, there was a general feeling that the Irish League would be resumed. However, it was decided at a meeting of the former league clubs that the league should not in fact operate for the 1918/19 season. Celtic were then induced to join the Belfast and District League in place of Glenavon. The new season therefore started with Celtic contesting this competition along with Belfast United, Cliftonville, Distillery, Glentoran and Linfield.

The newcomers' absence from senior league football over the previous few seasons did not seem to have the least effect upon them. With all but one of the league games completed, they were in a commanding position at the top of the table, which read as follows:

	P	W	D	L	F	A	Pts
Belfast Celtic	9	7	1	1	15	6	15
Linfield	9	6	1	2	14	8	13

The top two teams met in the last match at Celtic Park. A crowd of 25,000 turned up to watch the encounter, which Celtic only had to draw to lift the league title. The Linfield team spoiled the party, however, as they scored the only goal of the match. With both teams now level on points, a test match was needed to find the outright winners.

The defeat by Linfield had only postponed the celebrations. In the test match, Celtic registered the only score of an exciting game. Danny McKinney struck a well-taken goal after McKee had blocked a Jimmy Ferris header. Celtic were therefore the champions in the first and only Belfast and District League campaign in which they participated.

The City Cup competition also saw Celtic finish equal top, this time with Glentoran. A test match in May failed to resolve the issue, the game ending in a 1-1 draw. Unfortunately, the game was marred by unsavoury acts of hooliganism. Rather than risk a repetition of such scenes in a replay, the administrators decided in their wisdom that the trophy should be held jointly by both teams.

On September 1st, 1919, the Irish League resumed after a four-year absence. Bohemians and Shelbourne rejoined the six members of the now defunct Belfast and District League. Celtic got off to a great start in the re-formed league. In the

Jimmy Ferris

first match of the season they defeated Glenavon, who had replaced Belfast United, by three goals to nil. All three goals came from Steve Mulholland, a Celtic hero of earlier days.

Celtic travelled to Dublin the following week for a match against Bohemians. The rampant Celts scored four goals to no reply. Another hat-trick was registered, this time by the great Jimmy Ferris, who was to join Mickey Hamill in the Irish International side in this season. Already the Celtic following began to talk about this being a league-winning team. They were not to be disappointed. The team continued on its winning way, and eventually won the championship with ease, winning ten and drawing three of their fourteen games. The figures speak for themselves:

P	W	D	L	F	L	Pts
14	10	3	1	27	6	23

Of the 27 goals scored, 14 were shared equally by Ferris and Mulholland. Kelly, Kerr and Burns scored a couple each, while McKinney, Grace, McLaughlin and Barrett all got their names on the score-sheet once. The other three goals went to captain Mickey Hamill.

Mickey had played a major role in the league-winning team of 1914/15, and once again he was vital to the present team's success. Week after week he played like a giant, making a nonsense of his 5 foot 8 stature, as he encouraged his team-mates when things were going wrong, and exhorted them to keep their concentration when they were leading. But most of all Mickey led by example. When the need arose, he would play at full-back one week, and turn out as an inside-forward the next.

The real success of this team, though, rested with the goalkeeper and two full-backs. Any defence that conceded only six goals in 14 games cannot be ignored. Before the season had begun, Elisha Scott had been signed up by Liverpool. He was replaced by a man who was well-known at Celtic Park, Scott's cousin Bertie Mehaffey. In the 14 league games, Bertie kept 9 clean sheets; and quickly re-established himself as a favourite of the Celtic fans.

Bertie's job was made considerably easier by the reassuring presence of full-backs Tom McDade and Fred Barrett. Tom was a very steady left-back, who was normally more than a match for the opposition's right-wing, but it was right-back Fred who was the outstanding player of the team. He was at his best in crucial matches against Celtic's rivals for the league title. He was magnificent in a 1-0 defeat of Glentoran which virtually ensured Celtic the championship. It was in this match, in fact, that Fred scored his only goal in the league campaign.

Others who played a part in this league-winning team included half-backs Mulligan, Norwood and Fergie, and forwards Smith, Hastie, Wishart, Harris and Devlin.

Regrettably, this season was marred by some deplorable scenes of crowd violence. The worst incident took place on St. Patrick's Day at Cliftonville, in a replayed Cup semi-final match between Celtic and Glentoran.

After the match had been abandoned due to crowd trouble, a maniac produced a revolver and proceeded to shoot it into the stand full of Glentoran supporters. As a result, four people had to be treated in hospital for serious gunshot wounds. Nor were these the only injuries inflicted. Many more were trampled underfoot in a frenzied rush for the exits after the shooting started. The police rushed in the direction of the shots to arrest the culprit. They were successful - the man was arrested, handcuffed and taken away in a police van under armed guard.

There were bound to be repercussions, of course, and these came at the next Appeals Committee.

After considering the referee's report, it was decided that Celtic should take no further part in the cup competition that year. It was further decided that they should be suspended from football for a month. The Celtic directors sensationally threatened to take the matter of the suspension to the High Court. They argued that, as the match had been played at a neutral venue, the Belfast Celtic club was not responsible for crowd behaviour.

A further bombshell was dropped by the same directors some weeks later, with the news that they intended to quit league football, and had made their players available for transfer. It was only when the share-holders urged the directors to reconsider their decision that they changed their minds. The action against the IFA was settled out of court to the satisfaction of both parties, and it was anticipated that Celtic would have a team in the next season's competitions.

What no-one could have anticipated was the terrible violence which was to break out on the streets of Belfast that summer. Although troubled times had in fact been foreseen by some, the extent of the violence which actually transpired went beyond the fears of even the gloomiest forecaster. It was impossible for normal life to continue, and sport was one of the many casualties.

Although the Irish League did continue, it was clear that the presence of Celtic and the two Dublin clubs would only cause further friction in an already tense situation. The League Management Committee therefore reluctantly gave Celtic, Bohemians and Shelbourne permission to withdraw from football until such times as the situation improved. It was to take another four years for that to happen.

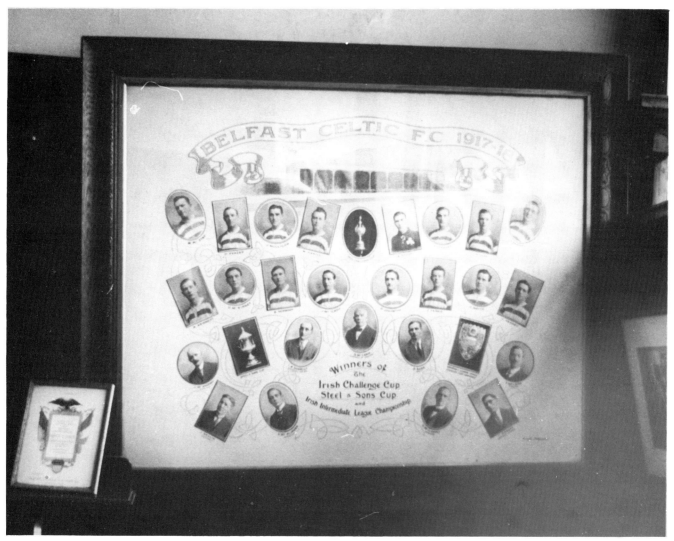

The Boardroom displays its heroes

These scenes were typical of the huge crowds which followed Belfast Celtic, whether home or away.

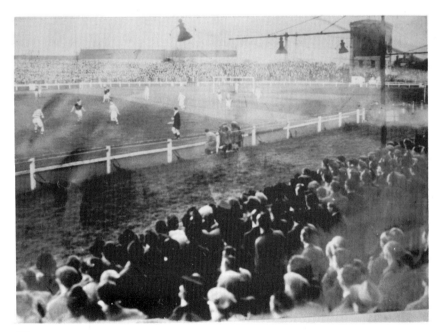

PART TWO

Austin's Team

1924 - 1934

Belfast Celtic 1924/25

Back Row *(left to right): Gamble, Fulton, Kirkwood, Ferguson, Pollock, McDowell.*
Front Row*: Gault, Moore, Kinsella, Ferris (Captain), Smith, S. Mahood, J. Mahood.*

I

The Glory Days Begin — 1924-1928

WHEN Celtic re-entered the football scene in 1924, it was with a completely new team. All the former players had moved to other clubs: Barrett and Ferris had been signed by Chelsea, while Hamill returned to Manchester, this time to play with City. He was joined there by Mulligan, Carroll and Kelly. The other members of the 1920 championship-winning team had joined various Irish League clubs.

Manager Austin Donnelly and trainer Joe Devlin were faced, then, with a formidable challenge, as they embarked upon the task of moulding a new pool of inexperienced players into a first-class football team.

Austin Donnelly, Chairman of the Board

Celtic's very first match of the season - away to Glenavon - was a remarkable occasion. Over 1,000 supporters followed the team to Lurgan, with almost half that number having to be turned away at the railway station. As on the first occasion when the two teams had met in Lurgan, the match was accompanied by a festive atmosphere.

The fans were well-rewarded for their loyal support, for they had the privilege of witnessing for the first time one of the best left-wing partnerships in Celtic's history. This came in the form of two of the smallest, but cleverest players in the league, Stanley Mahood and his brother Jackie, the 'Mighty Atom'. Mrs Mahood's two 'wee sons' were to become a force in Irish football over the next half-dozen years. In this first match, Stan scored twice in a 3-1 Celtic victory.

The young Celtic team continued to surprise and delight their supporters throughout the season. In the fifth game of the league programme, a large crowd turned up at Celtic Park to watch the match against old rivals Linfield. In a magnificent encounter, which contained some sparkling play from both teams, Celtic emerged as winners by the odd goal in three. The first goal came from centre-forward Andy Smyth, while Stan Mahood scored the second. These two were Celtic's top marksmen in the league.

The team received a great boost half-way through the season when Jimmy Ferris returned to Celtic Park. Like the Mahoods, Jimmy was central to the Celtic success of the next few seasons, as was the genial Sammy Moore. Sammy started out as an outside-right, but was later to make the right-half position his own.

By the time the league finished, Celtic were in a very creditable third place with 27 points.

In the same season, the directors continued their fine work of making Celtic Park one of the most comfortable enclosures in Ireland, by having a stand built on the unreserved side of the ground. Perhaps the most pleasing aspect of the season was the atmosphere of sportsmanship which prevailed. Thankfully, there was no repeat of the crowd violence that had existed in Celtic's last season, and the keen but friendly rivalry which was evident on the pitch extended to the terraces.

While the new Celtic team had done very well in their first season back in football, not even the most optimistic supporter could have predicted the success that was to come their way in 1925/26. This was to go down as the most successful season in the Club's history.

In the close season, the directors had pulled off a tremendous coup with the signing of Sam Curran, a prolific centre-forward who had scored 50 goals for junior team Woodburn in each of the previous two seasons. Although he had been the target of other top clubs, Sam was obviously attracted to the set-up at Celtic Park. The Celtic supporters looked to great things from the Carrick man, and they were not to be disappointed.

Joe Devlin, Celtic's Physiotherapist

Another shrewd acquisition was that of outside-right Jack McGrillen. Along with Ferris, Curran and the two Mahoods, he was part of one of the most formidable forward lines that the Irish League has ever produced. Jack had served his football 'apprenticeship' in the Falls Park League, which also produced the excellent full-back partnership of Bob Ferguson and Bertie Fulton.

Celtic started the league well, and by the end of September were in a healthy second place. But just a month later they were a poor third, four points behind leaders Distillery, and three behind Glentoran.

The second half of the season was a completely different story. Scoring at the rate of three goals a match, Celtic were almost unbeatable, winning 10 out of 11. In the end, they emerged as champions by the comfortable margin of three points. Austin Donnelly had succeeded in putting together a league-winning team in less than two seasons.

Sam Curran certainly lived up to his reputation as a goal-scorer, with 18 league goals. But Sam's limelight was stolen to a large extent by the 'wee man' on the left wing, Jack 'the Giant Killer' Mahood, who notched up 14 goals in 18 league matches, a magnificent feat for a winger. Brother Stan had not been idle either - he got in on the act with nine goals of his own.

The Irish League Trophy was the first of five to end up in the Celtic Park

Stanley Mahood

Jack Mahood

There is a team called Celtic,
They are always to the fore;
They've won their share of trophies,
And are keen to win some more.
Jack Diffen, always spiffin',
Hamill and 'Fergie' grand;
Pollock, Moore and Inch
Are the best halves in the land.
McGrillen, Ferris, Curran,
We know they are the goods;
But best of all, when on the ball,
Are the famous two Mahoods.

As the poem suggests, the Mahood brothers were firm favourites at Celtic Park. The dynamic left-wing duo provided forwards like Curran with countless gilt-edged scoring chances.

They were also suberb marksmen in their own right. Indeed, 'Mighty Atom' Jack was the club's top scorer three seasons in a row - surely a record for an outside-left. His consistency gained him the first of his nine international caps in 1926.

Brother Stanley's clever footwork and accuracy were also a feature of the great team of the Twenties. As well as being a provider of goals for his team-mates, Stan himself scored over 100 times for Celtic before moving to Derry City in 1932.

Jack was transferred to Ballymena the following season. Ironically, his first match against his old team proved to be the last of his career. Jack broke a leg in a collision with Celtic keeper Tommy Breen. The fracture was so bad that he was never to play again.

boardroom that season. The next to be won was the Gold Cup. Celtic met Cliftonville in the final at Windsor Park. With the forwards in devastating form, Celtic ended up as easy 3-0 winners. The first was scored when little Stan Mahood fairly bundled the opposing keeper over the line. Jack McGrillen scored the second from a Jack Mahood cross, after the left winger had mesmerised the Cliftonville defence. Jack Mahood scored the third himself from a Curran pass.

Celtic won the City Cup in the same season, scoring 32 goals in 11 games. Exactly half of these were scored by Curran, to add to his 18 league goals. Jackie Mahood also maintained his fine striking rate for the season, finding the net nine times.

Celtic's fourth trophy was the Charity Cup. They fought out a 1-1 draw with Glentoran in the final. Curran, of course, was the scorer. It was decided that the clubs should hold the Cup jointly.

While the League Championship trophy is the most important one, the Irish Cup is surely the most glamorous and coveted. Great Cup Finals have been remembered long after the league campaigns have fallen into oblivion. The Cup was therefore the trophy that the Celtic players and supporters most looked forward to winning.

Sam Curran again had his shooting boots on in the early rounds. He scored twice against Queen's Island and Glenavon, and got one of Celtic's three in the semi-final defeat of Newry. The scene was then set for a classic final encounter with Linfield at Cliftonville.

After an early Linfield goal, Celtic equalised when a long-range shot from George Perry was dropped by the Linfield keeper. As the ball rolled over the line, Sam Curran stepped in to help it on its way. Linfield scored soon after, to give them a 2-1 half-time lead.

The score stayed the same until nine minutes from the end. Then Sam Curran took over. He quickly exploited a gap in the Linfield defence, burst through it, and scored with an unstoppable shot. A few minutes later Sam made another lightning dash, and finished with a well-taken shot to score the winning goal.

It had been a uniquely successful season. Curran's final goal tally was a record-breaking 57, which included 6 in representative games for the Irish League and full International team. The diminutive Mahoods had also played their parts on the left, with Jack also winning his first international cap. Jack McGrillen also did sterling work on the right-wing, and was to be rewarded the following season with a cap against Scotland.

Jimmy Ferris had a profound influence on the younger members of the team. As one reporter so rightly put it, Jimmy was the 'cog upon which the Celtic

Sammy Curran

In the summer of 1925, Austin Donnelly brought one of the hottest goal-scoring properties in Irish football to Celtic Park. The question was, could Sammy Curran live up to the reputation that he had established at Woodburn?

'Blind Sammy' didn't let Austin or the supporters down. In his first season, the big man from Carrick scored an Irish League record of 51 goals (plus 6 in international matches). He also scored a memorable hat-trick in the Irish Cup Final to turn a 1-2 half-time deficit against Linfield into a 3-2 victory.

Sammy was the supreme opportunist. 'If there is to be a spectacular goal recorded, you can always bet on Curran snatching it', wrote one admirer after he had scored a last-gasp equaliser against the Blues.

In December 1926, Sam set another record when he scored a hat-trick in EACH HALF against Newry.

In just 3 seasons, Sammy scored more than 170 goals for Celtic. He was the top marksman, not only in the Irish League, but throughout Europe.

After his spell with Celtic, Sammy joined Derry City in 1929 for their first season in the Irish league. He had the distinction of scoring Derry's first-ever League hat-trick, and was also the club's top scorer that season.

37

machinery revolved'. Though eventually slotting into the inside-right position, he was a true 'utility' player, who could play in any position on the field.

Captain Sammy Moore also deserves much of the praise. While the forwards were busy with their goal-scoring exploits, Sammy skillfully marshalled the young defence. Unlike the forward line, which had remained fairly settled throughout the season, the defence had undergone many changes. In an attempt to improve the 'goals against' record, five goalkeepers had been used - Smith, Doherty, Corscadden, Diffen and Fitzmaurice.

Bob Ferguson, Bertie Fulton, Billy Scott and Alf Bruce had all proved to be very competent full-backs. The Pollock-Moore-Perry combination was an effective half-back line, which was supplemented by Joe Kane and Billy Kirkwood.

To round off an almost perfect season, and to underline their superiority, Celtic travelled to Dublin where they played the FAI champions Shelbourne in a challenge match. They beat their southern challengers 4-2, with Moore, Curran and the two Mahoods scoring a goal each. Celtic thus assumed the undisputed title of 'All-Ireland Champions'.

Sammy Moore

In 1926/27 Celtic won the League Championship again, and in even more convincing style than in the previous season. They went through the entire programme without suffering a single defeat. In fact, the league race was all over by Boxing Day, when a 4-2 victory over Linfield gave the champions a virtually unassailable six-points lead. The five forwards, who had combined so effectively the year before, scored an average of three goals per game.

Sam Curran was again the supreme marksman, scoring 26 league goals. Towards the middle of the season, Sam actually went two matches without scoring. Some observers were beginning to wonder whether he had lost the magic touch. Obviously resenting any such suggestion, Sam answered his critics in the best possible manner - with his feet. Newry Town bore the brunt of his resentment, as he proceeded to put six goals past their unfortunate keeper in a 7-2 victory. By the end of the season, the centre-forward had scored 47 goals for Celtic, to add to his 51 of 1925/26. He now needed just two more for his century.

Sam chose what was described as 'one of the most eventful evenings in the history of the Belfast Celtic club' to score these goals. On Easter Monday, Celtic played their illustrious namesakes from Glasgow in a friendly at the Donegall Road ground. The Scottish Cup holders were expected to give their Belfast cousins a lesson in the art of football. But it was the Belfast team who won 4-2. In a fine match, Jack Mahood and Curran each scored twice, the biggest cheer going up when the latter scored his hundredth Celtic goal in only his second season.

Jackie McGrillen

Sam, of course, had the fine service from his fellow-players to thank for many of his goals. As well as the established forwards already mentioned, Celtic were fortunate to have an outstanding substitute in Tom Hanna from Ballymena. In Tom's first game, at outside-right for the injured Jack Mahood, he scored a great hat-trick in a 4-2 win over Glenavon. Tom scored seven goals in nine matches, and must count himself unlucky to have played at the same time as such talented players as Ferris, McGrillen and the Mahoods, with the result that he could not command a regular place in the team.

In the same match in which Hanna made his debut, a 'new' player occupied the centre-half position. This was none other than Mickey Hamill, back in the side after six years absence in Manchester and then Boston. Although older and perhaps just a shade slower, Mickey still played with all the poise and control of his younger days. On his return to the team, he formed a vital link between the defence and attack. His long, deliberate passes out from defence were like manna from heaven for the wingers.

Mickey's return to 'Paradise' did pose one problem for manager Donnelly. He now had five first-class half-backs at his disposal, any of whom could have been an automatic selection for any other team in the country. Austin finally plumped for a Moore-Hamill-Eddie Inch line-up. So Billy Pollock and George Perry were the unfortunate players to be side-lined.

The last line of defence also proved to be very sound. Jack Diffen established himself in goals, and he had the support of two able full-backs in Bob Ferguson and Billy Scott.

In the same season Celtic won the County Antrim Shield, the only senior trophy to have eluded them the year before. The final, against Junior team Dunmurry, was not the formality that everyone expected. Although Celtic scored first through Curran, the underdogs took a shock 2-1 lead early in the second half. The equaliser came when Stan Mahood tapped in a perfect McGrillen cross. Near the end, Sammy Curran latched on to a Hanna pass and beat the Dunmurry keeper with a low, hard drive. The result, then, was a narrow 3-2 win for Celtic.

If there were any doubts about Celtic's supremacy in Irish League football, they were dispelled the next season, 1927/28. Not only did the team emulate the league successes of the previous two seasons, but they actually surpassed them in terms of goal-scoring consistency.

Austin Donnelly's only problem at the beginning of the season was in filling the right-back position, which had been vacated by the departure of Billy Scott to the English club Lancaster Town. But the problem of finding a suitable partner for Bob Ferguson was not a crucial one, for in that season Celtic played most of their football in the opponents' half of the field.

The forwards were as magnificent as ever. Curran attained the unthinkable by putting his scoring exploits of the past two seasons into the shade. The big man from Carrick had chalked up his half-century for the season by the end of January, and went on to score another couple of dozen by May. With the Mahoods, Ferris and McGrillen also in top goal-scoring and goal-creating form, the great Celtic machine rolled relentlessly along throughout the season.

With half-a-dozen league matches still to be played, it was obvious that Celtic would win the championship for the third successive season. The only question now was whether they could top the 100 goal mark in the league, a remarkable average of almost four a game.

In the last league game of the season Celtic needed to put four past Bangor at Celtic Park to reach that magic target. But what a shock when the seasiders went in at half-time with a 3-0 lead.

During the interval Austin Donnelly must have given his team a real tongue-lashing, for they were a different set of players in the second half. Curran quickly pulled a goal back, and then Jack Mahood scored twice to level the scores. With the famous 'war cry' ringing all around the stadium, there was a merciless onslaught on the Bangor goal as the Celtic forwards looked for number 100. Accompanied by a mighty cheer, the goal fittingly came to one of the club's most loyal and popular servants, Jimmy Ferris.

To round the evening off, Celtic went on to register a fifth goal. This was scored by another promising player, Pat Gallagher, who waited patiently in the wings throughout the season for his chance to play first-team football.

It was young Gallagher who set Celtic on the road to winning their second City Cup in three years. Playing at centre-forward, he scored a fine hat-trick in a 4-1 defeat of Ards. Jack McGrillen was in fine form in the same competition, hitting important winners against Cliftonville and Bangor, and netting a hat-trick against Coleraine. But yet again, most of the goal-scoring was done by the amazing Sam Curran, who got almost half of the 33 goals in the competition. Without a doubt, Sam was the hottest goal-scoring property in the British Isles at this time.

By devious ways where the exile strays
In many a land afar,
Their fancy flies to 'The Paradise',
No matter where they are;
The Green and White, like a beacon light
Upon their path has shone,
And the question slips from Celtic lips -
*   How did 'the boys' get on?*

(12 September, 1927 - poem in 'The Celt')

II

Four in a Row —1928-1929

In the early 1890's, when the Irish League was in its infancy, Linfield won the competition three years in succession. The same club repeated that feat from 1907 to 1909. No club had ever won four league titles in a row. It was with the aim of achieving this record that Celtic embarked upon a new season in August 1928.

Everyone was confident that the target would be achieved. The defence was strengthened by the return from London of Bertie Fulton, as Bob Ferguson's full-back partner. The half-back line was as strong as ever, with Pollock, Moore, Inch, Hamill and Pat Lennon all competing to fill the three positions.

Jack McGrillen had left in the close season to try his luck in America, but his place on the right wing was admirably filled by young Jim Carroll, a clever little Glaswegian. Keiller McCullough, who had scored some important goals the previous season, was ready to play his part. Curran, Ferris, Gallagher, Ned Weir and the two Mahoods were all still available to display their goal-scoring talents.

Seldom, if ever, could Celtic have begun a season with such a wealth of talent. If one player should lose his place on the team, there was always another to step straight in. With the possible exception of goalkeeper Jack Diffen, no-one could be certain of having his name on the team-sheet. It was this competition for the honour of wearing the green-and-white jersey, more than any other factor, which made the Celtic teams of this era so memorable.

To illustrate this point, we can look at the case of Sammy Curran. In the first match of the season, Sam was sent of in a bruising encounter with Ballymena. As a result, he was suspended for a month. While most other teams would greatly miss their central attacker and top scorer, Pat Gallagher was able to fill the gap.

In his first match as centre-forward, Pat scored a hat-trick in a 7-0 victory over Portadown. He then got a couple in a 7-1 defeat of Newry, and four when Celtic beat Larne by the same margin. He followed this by scoring twice against Ards and Cliftonville, and added another against Glentoran. It was only after Pat injured his ankle in his last match that Sammy was able to regain his place - about a month after his suspension had ended.

With only 9 games played, Celtic were already in a commanding position. In

Boardroom Pride

these matches, they scored an amazing 47 goals and conceded only three. All five forwards - Gallagher, Carroll, McCullough and the two Mahoods - scored in the 5-0 win over Cliftonville. The same five repeated the feat the following week when Glentoran were defeated 6-0.

The referee in the Glentoran match, Mr Fogg from Bolton, was clearly impressed by the Celtic display. 'I did not know there was such a great side in Ireland' he enthused. He went on to remark that, of the English Second Division sides, only Middlesborough was as good. He added that on the day's display Celtic would have beaten half-a-dozen English First Division clubs. Perhaps Mr Fogg was being generous to the English First Division.

With the forwards continuing to score with almost monotonous regularity, there was little doubt half-way through the season that Celtic were on their way to that record fourth successive title. The lowly Queen's Island had the misfortune of being the victims of a particularly frisky forward line one December afternoon.

With Celtic already nine goals in front, scored by Jack Mahood (5), Curran (3) and Stan Mahood, Stan and Jack decided that it was time for Jimmy Ferris to add his name to the score-sheet. They therefore passed the ball between themselves on the edge of the penalty area, while they waited for Jimmy to come up and do the honours. He duly obliged, strolling up to receive the ball and nonchalantly walking it into the net for number 10.

The prolific scoring of the Celtic forwards made the previous season's league total of 101 look positively dismal. The hundredth goal was scored with five games to spare, in a 4-0 defeat of Bangor,and they went on to add a further 16 to the total.

The only remaining challenge was to emulate the feat of the 1926/27 team by going through the league programme undefeated. A potential stumbling-block to the achievement of this objective were arch-rivals Linfield, in the third last match. A large crowd gathered at Celtic Park, most of them wearing green-and-white, to witness the encounter on a rainy February afternoon. They were rewarded by one of Celtic's biggest wins over Linfield, as they scored five goals without reply. Big Sam Curran scored 4 times, and left-back Billy Pollock got the fifth. The result put Celtic eight points ahead of their rivals, and of course ensured that the championship trophy went yet again to Celtic Park.

Manager Austin Donnelly, always so impassive and inscrutable, showed in his own way just how much importance he placed on the Linfield result. He took the match ball, cleaned it carefully, and simply said 'Money wouldn't buy that ball'. Thus Austin summed up the dreams and achievements of his five years as manager.

But the greatest drama in the league campaign was reserved for the last match against Glentoran. With the score level at 2-2, the Glens were awarded a penalty. It looked as if the unbeaten record was about to be relinquished at the very last hurdle. The circumstances of the penalty were bizarre, to say the least. For perhaps the only time ever in the history of soccer, the referee awarded a penalty against the keeper for hand-ball.

It happened like this: towards the end of the match Jack Diffen came off second best in a collision with an upright. He was helped off the pitch in a concussed state, and Pat Gallagher donned the keeper's jersey. But when Jack realised that his defence was under great strain, he rushed back onto the field, wearing Pat's jersey, to resume goals. Before jerseys could be exchanged, a shot came in from a Glens' forward, which Jack instinctively saved. The referee, still looking upon Gallagher as goalkeeper, immediately awarded a penalty to Glentoran. Nor did the drama end there; Glentoran's Allen took a well-placed penalty, which seemed to be destined for the corner of the net, until Diffen, concussion and all, flung himself at the ball and managed to save it. The cheer that greeted this incredible save was the biggest of the season. Because of it, the undefeated record was intact.

Few managers in football could have equalled the achievements of Austin Donnelly.

During the summer of '24, he put together a team 'from scratch'. That team finished third in the Irish League in its first season. The following season, and the three after that, Austin's Celtic were Irish League Champions. They had re-written the record books in the process. In the 74 league games between 1926-29, they had lost only once. They had been undefeated in two seasons, and had twice scored over 100 goals. Most important of all, they had won four league Championships in succession, something which had never been done before, and would only be equalled by the great Celtic team of the late Thirties.

The statistics themselves are eloquent testimony to the superiority of 'Austin's Team':

	P	W	D	L	F	A	Pts	Pos'n
1924/25	22	11	5	6	36	31	27	3rd
1925/26	22	16	1	5	52	38	33	1st
1926/27	22	15	7	0	66	36	37	1st
1927/28	26	20	5	1	101	35	45	1st
1928/29	26	22	4	0	116	23	48	1st

The season did bring some disappointment to the Celtic following. After a 3-0 victory over Linfield in the Cup semi-final, Celtic were hot favourites to beat

Ballymena in the final, in the latter club's first year in Senior football. However, it has been proved time and again that Cup football can be as unpredictable as the Irish weather. Ballymena were 2 goals up after 47 minutes, and although Jack Mahood pulled one back, the men from the Braid kept their heads and held on for a well-deserved victory.

In the close season, Celtic accepted an invitation from the Danish F.A. to visit Copenhagen, where they played three matches. The results were nothing to write home about - a draw followed by two defeats - but everyone concerned with the tour had a thoroughly enjoyable time. A holiday in the clean, smoke-free air of the Danish capital was a fitting reward for the players who had left an indelible impression on the history of Irish football.

Chris Fitzmaurice (top left), Billy Scott,
Billy Pollock (bottom) - stalwarts of the great
1925/29 team.

45

Wall of Fame

III

Years of transition — 1929-1934

Celtic began the 1929/30 season under a new manager, with Archie Heggarty taking over the reins from Austin Donnelly. The team personnel also underwent some changes. Jack Diffen and Sam Curran left to play for Shelbourne and Derry City respectively, while Eddie Inch also left Celtic Park. The legendary Mickey Hamill, who had been plagued with a knee injury, decided that it was time to hang up his boots after 21 years in football.

But the saddest story of the season concerned Jimmy Ferris. Towards the season's end, Jimmy went to the doctor complaining of 'flu'. On checking him, the doctor found that Jimmy had a serious heart complaint, and advised him to give up the game immediately. He followed the doctor's advice, but like Mickey continued to be associated with the club in a scouting and advisory capacity.

With all the upheaval, it was no surprise that Celtic could not repeat the glorious results of the previous four years. However, the supporters were rewarded by a great City Cup run. By the time the thirteen-match programme was complete Celtic found themselves sharing the top spot with Glentoran.

The test match to find the outright winners was played in a cup-tie atmosphere at Grosvenor Park. In this match, a new Celtic star was found in Jack Coulter. The young centre-forward, who had been recruited from junior team Dunmurry, scored a magnificent hat-trick in a 3-1 Celtic victory. His first two goals were set up by the wingers, with Jack Mahood supplying the pass for the first, and Carroll the second. Jackie's third goal was a magnificent solo effort, as he weaved his way past the Glens' defenders and finished perfectly by coolly slotting the ball past the helpless keeper. Bertie Fulton's performance in defence caught the eyes of the Irish selectors, who awarded him the first of his twenty caps in this season.

The City Cup was retained by Archie Heggarty's team the following season. This time there was no need for a test match, as the Celts went through the 13-match programme undefeated, scoring at the rate of four goals a match. Jack Mahood found himself as top scorer in the competition with 13 goals. He was followed by Jack Coulter in 10, while brother Stan chipped in with 8.

Jack Diffen made a welcome return from Shelbourne, and played in all but one of the City Cup games, conceding only 10 goals. His consistency earned him a cap against Wales. The result of an excellent all-round team effort brought about the following commendable City Cup figures:

P	W	D	L	F	A	Pts
13	10	3	0	52	12	23

For the second year in succession, Jack Mahood emerged as Celtic's top scorer with 33 goals, to add to his 43 of the previous season. Jack's goal-scoring exploits over the year prompted the writer of 'The Celt', the club's official programme, to remark that the left-winger's goals were as numerous as the sands at Ballyholme.

The 1931/32 season was a time of transition for Celtic. Many young players were being given the chance to prove themselves in senior football, and the seeds of the great team that was to dominate the late Thirties were already being sown.

Among these were goalkeeper Tommy Breen, whose spectacular and fearless style that was to be his hallmark was already in evidence. Then there were the two Donnellys, outside-right Tom from Dundalk, and left-winger Joe from Newry. Inside-right Jackie Brown also proved to be a fine acquisition.

The best signing of all was that of Davy 'Boy' Martin from Cliftonville. This ex-soldier with the Royal Ulster Rifles had already begun to establish a reputation as a goal-scorer, a reputation that was to be greatly enhanced over the years. Davy sounded a warning to all opposition goalkeepers when, in his debut for Celtic, he scored both their goals in a 2-2 draw with Derry.

So there was no despondency in the Celtic camp at the end of the season. And in the last game, the Charity Cup final, Celtic gained a meritorious victory over old rivals Linfield.

Having laid the foundations of a successful team, Archie Heggarty handed over the running of the club to genial Scotsman Jimmy McColl. Jimmy tasted immediate success as he witnessed his team win the League championship for the first time in 4 years.

Once Davy Martin hit his first goal against Distillery, his name was a permanent feature on the score-sheet. His league goals included hat-tricks against Bangor, Glentoran and Ards, and four against Cliftonville and Larne.

Davy scored 36 league goals in all. He was well-served by the left-wing partnership of Jack Mahood and Joe Donnelly, Jack's brother Stan having moved to Derry City. Besides supplying Davy with scoring opportunities, Jack helped himself to a dozen goals, while Joe scored eleven. Jack Coulter, Keiller, McCullough, Jack Brown and Billy Firth all contributed to the team's success from the right-wing. Tommy Breen established himself in goals, while Alex Wright, Bertie Fulton, Bob Ferguson, Sammy Moore, Billy Pollock and Bob Turley all defended well.

Jackie Coulter, Celtic striker transferred to Everton

Belfast Celtic, 1932/33

Back Row *(left to right): J. Devlin, A. Wright, W. Pollock, T. Breen, J. Feenan, W. Firth, R. Ferguson.*
Front Row*: R. Barr, J. Donnelly, K. McCullough, D. Martin, R.P. Fulton, J. Coulter, J. Mahood, J. McColl.*

Just before Christmas 1932, the Celtic directors signed two 18-year-olds from Junior clubs Crusaders and Ballymoney. The first was Harry Walker, the other Peter O'Connor. These unknown teenagers were destined to be two of Celtic's finest and longest-serving players.

Harry got Celtic off to a great start in the City Cup competition. Deputising for Davy Martin, who was on international duty, he scored a hat-trick in a 4-2 win over Linfield. By the end of the programme, Celtic and Linfield found themselves on equal points at the top of the table. Celtic won the resulting test match 2-1, the goals coming almost inevitably from 'Boy' Martin. The first was an unstoppable shot from a Walker pass, the second a neat header from a Coulter cross.

Davy scored 73 goals in all during the season. He signed professional forms with the club in March, and celebrated his new status by scoring 5 goals in a 6-1 City Cup defeat of Larne. Perhaps he was being paid on a bonus system.

Celtic's prolific centre-forward started off the 1933/34 season as he had ended the previous one. He had already scored twelve goals in his first five matches, when he was called upon to lead the Irish attack in the Home International match in Scotland. Davy's two goals in the match, which gave Ireland a rare 2-1 win, earned him rave reviews in the cross-channel papers. One of them, the *Sunday Referee*, had the following to say about his performance:

'Ireland has discovered a wonderful young centre-forward, a boy in years but a veteran in football knowledge. Before the game was more than half over, Scottish critics and English club managers were raving about him. The lad is a football genius, an artist in ball control. His 'selling the dummy' had the Scottish defence in a constant tangle. He is a deadly shot, and he has the quick-thinking brain of the football tactician.'

Ireland's new hero had the opportunity to display the above qualities a week later, when Celtic met the English First Division club Sheffield United in a 'friendly' at Celtic Park. Sheffield brought with them Jimmy Dunne, Martin's rival for the centre-forward position in the Irish International team. This was the perfect occasion to make a comparison between the two.

In the event, there was simply no comparison. Dunne was totally ineffective against the centre-half John Feenan and his colleagues, while at the other end Davy, with the help of Jackie Coulter, another hero of the Scottish match, was tearing the English defence apart. He scored Celtic's first goal on the half-hour, heading home a perfect Coulter cross. Jack Brown supplied the cross from the other wing which resulted in Davy heading home his second goal. The hat-trick arrived when he thundered home a long-range shot.

Although overshadowed by the goal-scoring talents of Martin, Jack Coulter remained a firm favourite with the supporters. He played most of the season at the inside-left, but it was only when he moved to the left-wing that his true brilliance shone through.

Coulter was a totally committed player, a fact which often got him into trouble with the referees. When he was sent off for the second time in the season during a cup-tie at Ballymena, he sat in a dressing-room in a thoroughly disgusted mood.

It so happened that an Everton representative was at the match, and before he left the Showgrounds Jackie was an Everton player, having signed on the spot for a £2,750 fee. So ended his short but distinguished career with Celtic.

Even though Davy Martin scored 37 league goals, Celtic finished in only second place, behind a Joe Bambrick-inspired Linfield team. Davy finished the season with a goal tally of 66, almost half the club's total of 133.

At the end of the season Jimmy McColl moved back to Edinburgh on business, and resigned as team manager.

Everyone concerned with the club was sorry to see the friendly Scot leave, but every cloud has a silver lining, as the saying goes. Jimmy's successor was a man who was a legend in his own lifetime, who was to usher in a brand-new Golden Age in the history of Belfast Celtic, and who was to equal and then surpass the achievements of Austin Donnelly and his great team of the Twenties. That man was Elisha Scott.

The Belfast Celtic 'Rallying Song'.
What a grand old team to play for,
What a grand old Cup to win,
When you read their history
It's enough to make your heart's blood
thrill;
We don't care if the money's right or
wrong,
Damn the hair we care.
For we only know that there's going to be a
match
And the Belfast Celtic will be there.

The words changed slightly over the years,
but the spirit of the 'war cry' was always the
same. The above version appeared in 'The
Celt' in 1927.

Peter O'Connor

*In 1936 Joe Payne of Luton Town scored ten goals in a match against Bristol
Rovers - a British Isles record that most people thought would never be broken. But
broken it was, just five years later, by Belfast Celtic's centre-forward Peter
O'Connor. Glenavon goalkeeper Hugh Kelly - himself destined to become a Celtic
immortal - was on the receiving end of a 13-0 drubbing by Celtic. Peter O'Connor
claimed 'eleven' goals, with four coming in the first 30 minutes, and the other seven
after half-time, a remarkable feat (for the record Jack Leathem and Charlie
McIlroy were the other goal-scorers that day).*

PART THREE

Elisha's Team

1934 - 1949

Belfast Celtic 2nds 1934/35
Back Row (left to right): W. McDonnell, E. Scott, D. McCloskey, R. Barr, P. McGuigan.
Second Row: G. Murray, C. McIlroy, J. Doulaghan, H. Walker, W. McMillan, K. McAlinden, T. Lavery,
J. Ritchie, J. McAlinden, C. Smyth.
Front Row: H. McAlinden, M. O'Neill, W. Donaghy, A. Kelly, P. O'Connor, A. McGivern, S.B. Lecky, C. Murphy.

I

Scott's Unstoppable Machine — 1934-1939

IN the years that had elapsed between his departure from Celtic Park in 1919 and his return as player-manager in the summer of 1934, the name of Elisha Scott had become a household word. The great man had played with distinction in the Liverpool goals, and his memory is still cherished in that city which has seen so many sporting heroes. He had already played 28 times for Ireland and, although now on the wrong side of 40, was to gain a further three caps during his spell as Celtic manager.

Elisha saw his team start the season in devasting form, scoring 24 goals in the first five games. Again it was Davy Martin who grabbed all the headlines, scoring 13 of the 24 - four each against Newry and Distillery, and five against Ards in a 9-0 win.

Martin had struck up an almost telepathic understanding with Jackie Brown on the right-wing. It was no secret that a number of cross-channel clubs were anxious to sign both players. Before Christmas of this season, the pair were transferred to Wolverhampton Wanderers for the then handsome sum of £7,500. Davy's price alone was £5,750, more than double that of any other Irish player.

The transfer of two key players was bound to have an adverse effect on results, but it was obviously Scott's policy not to stand in the way of any player furthering his career.

Elisha himself had a personal disappointment when, in an international against Scotland (which Ireland won 2-1 with goals by Coulter and Martin), he broke three fingers. He was out of action for some months, but the quality of goalkeeping at Celtic Park did not suffer, as he was replaced by Tommy Breen, himself a custodian of international class.

The new manager had the satisfaction of bringing the Gold Cup back to Paradise after a long absence. A semi-final win over Ards set the stage for a final encounter with Linfield. In the final at Grosvenor Park, Celtic established a 2-0 half-time lead, with both goals coming from the head of outside-left Matty Geoghegan, a newcomer from Dublin.

The expected second-half comeback by Linfield did not materialise. Inspired by Davy Martin - he was not transferred until the following week - the Celtic attack proceeded to tear the Blues' defence apart. Davy scored the third after

Football.

MARTIN AND BROWN LEAVING CELTIC

Wolves Offer £7,500—Martin's Fee a Staggerer—Said to be £5,700— Derry Fall at Celtic Park

9/12/34

(BY "BEN MADIGAN")

The Celtic directors, after match time on Saturday sprang the greatest surprise in football transfers since Coulter went to Everton nine months ago—the proposed transfer of Martin and Brown to Wolverhampton Wanderers at a joint fee of £7,500.

Martin's price is said to be £5,750, and the figure mentioned in the case of Brown £1,750.

This sensational announcement dwarfed everything else in the way of gossip regarding the day's football, and few people took any notice of the fact that Derry City's 4—1 defeat at Celtic Park had made the League championship a certainty for Linfield.

Distillery surprised Glentoran with a 3—1 score at the Oval—the Baily macarretti team's first defeat of the season. It is good to see Mickey Hamill's team turn the corner. Their luck was too bad to last.

Linfield did all that was asked of them in a scrappy game at Lurgan, and won 3—1 by virtue of stronger second-half finish. Eckersley saved a penalty from Hewieson early in the second half when the teams were level at 1—1.

A Manchester United representative watched Newry's left-winger, Roberts, at Coleraine, where the home team, led by Craig, the Donacloney junior, won 4—1.

Syd Over was in rare form at Solitude, and scored five of Cliftonville's eight goals against Ards. The Ardsmen were outclassed but had two

Davy Martin

Martin and Brown sold for £7,500

Johnny Brown

Davy 'Boy' Martin

Davy Martin, the little drummer boy from the Royal Ulster Rifles, certainly made a big noise in his short spell at Celtic Park.

Once described as the greatest opportunist ever to have led an Irish forward line, he seemed to score goals at will in his two and a half seasons with the club.

After his transfer to Wolves, Davy continued to win International caps, both with the Molyneaux club and later with Nottingham Forest.

On the outbreak of war, he rejoined the RUR, and resumed his football career with Glentoran.

But it's as a dashing goal-scorer with Belfast Celtic that Davy 'Boy' Martin will always be remembered. In those dark depressing days of the early 1930's, he lifted the hearts of many a Celtic supporter with his breath-taking goals.

rounding international centre-half Jones with contemptuous ease. He added an easy fourth when finding himself unmarked inside the penalty area.

A most pleasing aspect of the season was the performance of the Celtic II team. Re-formed in 1929/30, and managed by Charlie Murphy, the Seconds had been Intermediate League Champions in 1931/32 and again two seasons later. In 1934/5 they had the rare distinction of winning all the Junior competitions for which they were eligible - the Intermediate League, Intermediate Cup, Steel and Sons Cup, Clements Lyttle Cup and McElroy Cup.

The Seconds also reached the final of the County Antrim Shield, when they put up a fine performance in a 4-2 defeat by Linfield. Celtic's scorers were the two Arthurs, Kelly and McGivern. Almost all of the team which played in the match were to graduate to first team football in the next few seasons. It consisted of Kevin McAlinden; Billy McMillen and Tom Lavery; Peter O'Connor, Jerry Murray and John Ritchie; Jimmy McAlinden, Willie Donaghy, Artie Kelly, Harry Walker and Arthur McGivern.

With such fine quality young players waiting for their chance to play for the Senior team, the future certainly looked very bright for Belfast Celtic Football Club.

It soon became clear that the club's hopes for the future were not misplaced. In the 1935/36 season, Celtic won the first of a long succession of League Championships. Manager Scott laid the foundations of success on a rock-steady and almost impregnable defence. Elisha himself kept goal for most of the season, keeping two of Ireland's keepers, Tommy Breen and Kevin McAlinden, in the reserves. Scott was 42 when he won his first Irish League medal, but it meant as much to him as any other honour in a long and distinguished career.

Left-back Bertie Fulton was as fresh as ever in this, his tenth season. Bertie won his fourth Championship medal this term, having been an integral part of the all-conquering team of the late Twenties. John Feenan showed great composure in the other full-back position.

The half-back line of Harry Walker, Jerry Murray and John 'Scotty' Walker proved to be a dominant force. Murray had been a member of the previous season's successful reserve side; he got his chance of a permanent berth in the Senior team when Keiller McCullough was transferred in November to Manchester City.

In his years with Celtic, Keiller's contribution to the team had been considerable. While the likes of Davy Martin and Jackie Coulter had been hitting the headlines, McCullough, either at right-half or inside-right, had been playing steadily and consistently. His consistency won him his first cap while still playing for Celtic, and he was to obtain further international honours while

"I canna' Give it to all of yiz"

Manager Elisha Scott continually told his players that if they were unmarked on the field and in a favourable position, they should shout for the ball in order to let the one in possession know where they were. During an exhibition match in Dublin, Celtic inside left Syd McIlroy was working his way steadily towards the opposing goal when the shouts began coming from the other forwards. "Over here, Syd." "Behind you, Syd." "Give it to me, Syd." McIlroy stopped in his tracks, put his foot on top of the ball and in that well-known mid-Antrim acent, snapped "I canna' give it to all of yiz."

at Maine Road. Keiller was one of the game's gentlemen, and he was a sad loss to the club.

While Elisha built his league-winning team on defence, the forwards went about their task of scoring the all-important goals. One young man to catch the imagination was the outside-right Norman Kernaghan. Norman was only seventeen, and his curly hair and impish face made him look even younger, but he played with a maturity beyond his years. Besides beating defenders and setting up chances for his team-mates, he scored 14 league goals himself. The following season he was to become one of Ireland's youngest-ever international players.

Magnus McPhee, and ex-Bangor and Dunfermline centre-forward, came into the team in mid-September. He finished the league campaign as Celtic's top scorer, with 16 goals. Matty Geoghegan was also on target ten times. The inside-forwards, Jimmy McKnight and Walter Bruce, completed the Championship winning line-up.

One of the most eagerly-awaited matches of the season was the County Antrim Shield Final. Celtic's opponents in this match were - Celtic II. The Seconds had won their third consecutive Intermediate League title, and had no intention of letting their senior colleagues dominate them in the final.

As is often the case, the actual occasion did not match the anticipation. The game was by no means a classic, and the only thing that separated the teams was a Willie Donaghy goal for the seniors. The 22 players on the Windsor Park pitch were:

Belfast Celtic: Breen; Feenan and Fulton; H. Walker, Murray and J. Walker; Kernaghan, McKnight, Kelly, Donaghy and Geoghegan.

Belfast Celtic II: K. McAlinden; McMillen and Lavery; O'Connor, Whiteside and Ritchie; J. McAlinden, Thompson, Shiels, Murphy and McGivern.

With such a wealth of talent at Celtic Park, it would seem that Elisha Scott had no need to look elsewhere to build up his already considerable success. Yet this is exactly what he did. 'Lish' set off in search of two key players, a centre-half and centre-forward. And he found two of the best in Jack Leathem and Jimmy Turnbull. As any centre-forward of the time could testify, big Jack was one of the best 'stoppers' around. He totally commanded the centre of the defence, and high crosses were invariably met by Jack 'The Hack's' head.

But it was Turnbull, the speedy goal-scoring machine from Geordie land, who had the greatest impact on Irish League football over the next few seasons. Jimmy had set an FAI scoring record of 66 goals with Cork City, and Elisha was hoping that he would produce that form for Celtic. His hopes were fully realised.

The Whatabouter

Elisha Scott was notorious for his lack of praise. No matter how good the team had played, or how many trophies they carried into the Celtic Boardroom, the Celtic manager was never satisfied and perhaps that was behind his unprecedented success. When his team defeated Glenavon by thirteen goals to nil and centre forward Peter O'Connor had broken the British record by scoring eleven goals in a single game, the players were sure that the icy shroud that enveloped Scott would finally melt. They were wrong. On entering the pavilion, O'Connor, with a grin that went from ear to ear, walked up to Scott. "Well, Boss," he said, "what do you think of that?" Scott's chiselled face remained impassive. Then he snapped "What about the three you missed?"

Tommy Breen

When the Newry Town goalkeeper came to Celtic Park in 1931, he faced the awesome challenge of filling the shoes of the legendary Elisha Scott. Drogheda-born Tommy Breen would eventually win the most fanatical of Scott worshippers to his side with almost twenty years of brilliance between the posts. Transferred to the English glamour club, Manchester United, in 1936, he was on course for an outstanding career when the Second World War intervened. He returned to Celtic for a couple of years before joining Linfield following a disagreement with the Donegall Road club. He had the grim prospect on more than one occasion of leading the Blues out at Celtic Park before his Falls Road neighbours, and on coming out of Mass on Sunday morning from St Paul's he would meet the usual banter with unfailing good humour.

His strength as the last line of defence lay in his uncanny judgement, particularly with the high ball, and his almost suicidal courage in coming out to meet an onrushing attacker. His own defenders also often felt the whiplash of his tongue should they stray out of position and leave him unprotected.

Breen's total of nine international caps is somewhat misleading as he reached the pinnacle of his career at a time when international football had been suspended. Yet he is remembered as one of the greatest of all goalkeepers and the hero of some of the greatest Belfast Celtic elevens.

Opposing defences had no answer for the sheer speed, strength and opportunism of the centre-forward. His goal-scoring was nothing short of phenomenal. He chalked up no fewer than nine league hat-tricks, excluding the six goals he put past the Ards goalkeeper in a 10-0 win. The records of Curran and Martin were smashed as Jimmy scored 43 league goals in his first season, exactly half the number scored by the club. By the end of the season, he had amassed a remarkable 82-goal total.

To coincide with Turnbull's arrival, inside-right Jimmy McAlinden was promoted to the first team after a spell in the reserves. His tricky footwork was a delight to watch, and his combination with winger Kernaghan was a feature of the season. On the other wing another useful partnership was flourishing in Walter Bruce and Charlie McIlroy, a 21-year-old signing from Ballymena.

The defence, too, had one of its most important seasons. Tommy Breen was almost unbeatable in goals - Scott having finally decided to 'hang up his boots' - and it was no surprise when he was snapped by Manchester United in mid-season. Kevin McAlinden stepped into the position vacated by Tommy, and was equally impressive.

Tom Lavery became established at right-back after John Feenan was transferred to Sunderland. Tom slotted perfectly into the defence beside captain Fulton, who by now was collecting medals like the Aga Khan collected horses. In the half-back line, Leathem's dominance was complemented by the skills of the two Walkers. With such a well-balanced team, success inevitably came Celtic's way. They won 20 and drew 4 of their 26 league games to easily retain the Championship. They added to this the County Antrim Shield and the Charity Cup. In the former, Turnbull scored the goal in a 1-0 defeat of Glentoran; in the latter Artie Kelly, the reserve centre-forward, was the scorer as Distillery were beaten by the same margin. But of all the matches played in the 1936/37 season, it is the Cup Final which is most remembered.

Celtic faced Linfield at the Oval in the Final. Fulton and Jimmy McAlinden missed the match through injury, but Billy McMillen and Pat McArdle stepped up from the seconds to replace them, and played as well as anyone.

Well as the rest of the team played, though, this match belonged to just one man. In the years to come, it was always referred to as the 'Jimmy Turnbull Final'. And what better stage for the 'goal machine' to display his remarkable talents, than in the most prestigious match of the year?

The Blues' defence was hopelessly vulnerable to Turnbull's speed, and his cool clinical finishing. His first goal came in just five minutes, and when he added a second after an hour, the Linfield challenge was virtually ended. But

60

Jimmy Turnbull

Like Sammy Curran some ten years earlier, Jimmy Turnbull came to Celtic Park in the summer of '36 with a reputation as a goal-scorer. And also like Sammy, it was a reputation that he fully lived up to.

Jimmy didn't just make an impact in his first season in the Irish League - he virtually exploded onto the scene. His tally of 82 goals was a club record that remained unbeaten throughout Celtic's existence.

Like Curran, the Gateshead man capped an unforgettable season by netting a superb hat-trick in the Cup Final against old rivals Linfield.

Turnbull was the leading scorer in the Irish League two years in succession. His statistics make envious reading for today's so-called strikers, who are called 'prolific' if they top 30 goals in a season:

Season	League	City Cup	IFA Cup	Antrim Shield	Gold Cup	Total
1936/37	43	17	7	9	6	82
1937/38	36	10	5	7	4	62
		Total for 2 Seasons				144

Belfast Celtic v Glenavon during the Gold Cup Semi-Final at Grosvenor Park. Celtic's goalkeeper Kevin McAlinden holds a fast shot while centre-half Charlie Currie looks on.

Bertie Fulton

Jimmy was still not finished; a couple of minutes from the end he nipped in to score his third goal for a memorable hat-trick.

The Celtic side, whose teamwork was as much a feature as Turnbull's goals, contained McAlinden; McMillen and Lavery; H. Walker, Leathem and J. Walker, Kernaghan, McArdle, Turnbull, Bruce and McIlroy.

Meanwhile Charlie Murphy's seconds were not to be outdone by the senior team. They picked up their fourth successive Intermediate League, won the Intermediate Cup for the third year in a row, and added the Clements Lyttle and McIlroy Cups.

Elisha Scott was evidently satisfied with his successful team, as he kept the same line-up for 1937/38. The understanding that had built up among the team members continued to grow, as they set about presenting their manager with his third league title in as many years.

For the second year running, Jimmy Turnbull was the top scorer in the Irish League with 36 league goals and 62 in all competitions. His goals included a club record of seven in the last game of the season, an 8-0 thrashing of Cliftonville. The same wing partnership as in the previous season contributed to the 88-goal total, while the defence was just as effective as before.

The winning of the league was not all plain sailing, however. Indeed Celtic shared first place with Derry City, and had to resort to a test match before they were allowed to keep the trophy.

The first test resulted in a 2-2 draw, with Harry Walker scoring from the penalty spot and Jack Leathem heading home a cross - something which was becoming part and parcel of the big man's game. Celtic made no mistake in the replay at Windsor. Although they were a goal down to the Brandywell team at half-time, goals from Bruce, Kernaghan and another Walker penalty ensured them that Elisha's men achieved the trio of championship wins.

Not only did Celtic retain the league title, they also held on to the Cup.

The final against Bangor went to a replay after a goal-less draw. Artie Kelly replaced the injured Turnbull, who had scored in each of the previous rounds. But the top scorer was not greatly missed, as Celtic had an easy 2-0 win. The first goal, and the highlight of the final, was a fine solo effort from Jimmy McAlinden. The second came from Walter Bruce, the other inside-forward. Apart from Kelly and the fit-again Fulton and McAlinden in place of McMillen and McArdle, the successful team was the same as in the previous season's final.

Back in 1932, Peter O'Connor and Harry Walker joined Celtic as teenagers. Harry had quickly established himself in the first team, and for the past few years had been the automatic choice at right-half.

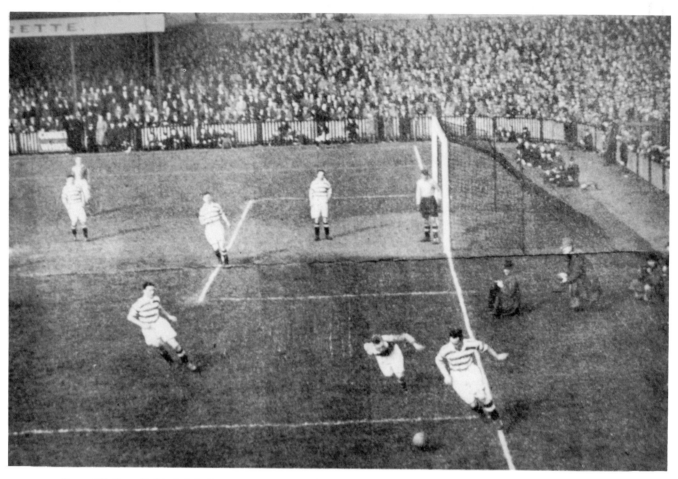

Scotty Walker, Celtic left-half, clears his lines during the 1937 Irish Cup Final against Bangor at Solitude.

Peter, meanwhile, had been playing a vital role in the success of Celtic II. He was the team captain throughout the Second's trophy-winning years. One of the reasons why Peter had not played many senior games was Charlie Murphy's reluctance to release him from second team duty. All that was to change dramatically in 1938/39.

O'Connor's opportunity came when Jimmy Turnbull sustained an injured foot. In what can only be described as a flash of inspiration, Scott decided to play the versatile young footballer at centre-forward. The experiment was an immediate success; Peter just could not stop scoring. The goals came thick and fast; three against Bangor, Derry and Coleraine; four against Cliftonville, six against Bangor the second time around.

The score in each of the last two matches mentioned was 10-1. Besides O'Connor's sharp-shooting, Norman Kernaghan scored hat-tricks in both matches. Norman had his best season to date, scoring 21 league goals from the right wing. Norman's partner, Jimmy McAlinden, was also playing the best football of his career. This fact was noticed by the international selectors, who awarded him his first cap against Wales. It was noticed, too, by the representatives of English club Portsmouth, to which Jimmy was transferred in mid-season.

With Bruce and McIlroy also in fine form, Celtic totalled 97 league goals, which brought back memories of the record-breaking team of ten years earlier. For the third year in succession, the defence contained the same personnel. Kevin McAlinden was injured and was out for a long spell, but Andy Jellie or Lloyd Armstrong were good deputies.

Not surprisingly, Celtic won the league with consummate ease. Elisha's men had now equalled the wonderful record of four successive championships set by Austin Donnelly's team of the Twenties. The question now on everyone's lips was - could they improve on it?

Three more senior trophies were added to the collection in 1938/39. The first was the Gold Cup, the first trophy Scott had brought to Celtic Park just four years earlier. Celtic won this by virtue of a 2-1 defeat of Glenavon, with Jimmy McAlinden and Walter Bruce scoring the all-important goals. Glentoran were beaten by the same margin in the County Antrim Shield Final. This time O'Connor got both the Celtic goals, bringing his total for the season past the 50 mark.

Finally, Celtic beat Linfield 1-0 in the last match of the season to lift the Charity Cup. Kernaghan scored the goal to add to his 33 for the season.

Norman Kernaghan

An Inter-League cap at the age of seventeen; fifty-four goals in one season; a star in three different positions and a hat-trick in four minutes. These are just some of the incredible records of Norman Kernaghan, Celtic outside-right during the glory years. Kernaghan was discovered by Austin Donnelly while still a schoolboy and playing at centre-half for the International youth side. His blinding speed, perfect ball control and powerful shot combined to make him one of the most feared forwards in the country.

He was still only seventeen when he faced the giants of football such as Frank Swift, Raich Carter, Ted Drake and Roy Westwood, and no winger in British football has ever approached his incredible 54 goals in one season.

In one unforgettable encounter against Larne, with Celtic trailing by three goals to one, Elisha Scott switched the little red-haired winger to centre-forward and Kernaghan responded by scoring three goals in four minutes - a feat which drew headlines in the major English newspapers the following day.

He never had any desire to enter English football, though many enticing offers were made and he spent his professional career with Belfast Celtic. He later became mamager of the Irish International Youth XI.

Belfast Celtic, 1936/37

Back Row (left to right): D. McClosky (Director), W. McMillan, H. Walker, J. Leathem, K. McAlinden, J. Walker, J. McAlinden, T. Lavery, A. Donnelly (Director), J. Devlin (Trainer).
Front Row: R. Barr (Secretary), N. Kernaghan, P. McArdle, J. Turnbull, R.P. Fulton (Captain), W. Bruce, C. McIlroy, M. O'Neill, E. Scott (Manager).

Belfast Celtic, 1939/40

Back row (left to right): E. Scott (Manager), J. Fitzpatrick (Director), J. Devlin (Trainer).
Middle row: H. Walker. W. McMillan, T. Breen, J. Vernon, K. McAlinden, J. Leathem, M. McWilliams.
Front row: A. Donnelly (Director), N. Kernaghan, J. McAlinden, R.P. Fulton, P. O'Connor, S. McIlroy, P. Nelson, R. Barr (Secretary).

II

Five in a Row — 1939-1940

The 1939/40 season was one of great anticipation. The club's players and officials were embarking on a great journey into the pages of history - a fifth successive League title. They sounded a warning to all pretenders to their crown in the opening City Cup competition.

This was the first time that the season began with the City Cup. In the previous years it had degenerated into a meaningless end-of-season series of matches, in which the public took little interest. By bringing it forward, the organisers hoped to restore its reputation.

Peter O'Connor resumed at centre-forward with the result that Turnbull returned to Cork where he could be sure of first-class football. 'Scotty' Walker also went home to Edinburgh. This enabled Jack Vernon to establish himself in the first team at centre-half, with Leathem moving to his left. The big Springfield Road man was destined to be one of the finest number 5's who ever wore a Celtic shirt. He was totally dedicated, brave and uncompromising. His greatness was recognised when he was picked to captain Great Britain in a match against the rest of Europe after the war.

By the end of the thirteen-match City Cup programme, Celtic were equal top with Derry. In the deciding test match, Derry were in the unfortunate position of finding Celtic in their most devastating form. Celtic won the match 7-1. O'Connor, who had scored 14 goals in the competition itself, added four more, while Kernaghan scored twice. The seventh came from Artie Kelly, who had established himself at inside-right after some years in the reserves.

The only match that Celtic lost in the City Cup was to Derry, at the beginning of September. For the next six months the Celtic supporters forgot what it was like to see their team lose a match. They remained undefeated in all competitions until the following March - a total of 36 matches. During this record-breaking run, they retained the Gold Cup, beating Linfield 1-0 in the final with a Kernaghan goal.

For the assault on their fifth championship in a row, Celtic's panel was strengthened by the return of two 'exiles'. On the outbreak of war, all football activities in England were terminated. Tommy Breen and Jimmy McAlinden came back from Manchester and Portsmouth, and re-formed their association with their old team.

Jimmy immediately resumed his right-wing partnership with Norman Kernaghan. Tommy's return was especially welcome, as it coincided with a recurrence of Kevin McAlinden's cartilage trouble. The Celtic team for most of the league campaign read: Breen; McMillen and Foulton; Walker and Leathem; Kernaghan, McAlinden, O'Connor, Kelly and McIlroy.

With such a perfect blend of sound defence and live-wire attack Celtic positively galloped away from their rivals in the league race. They went through the first 18 games without defeat, scoring at a rate of four goals a game, and culminating in a 12-0 defeat of Newry - a new Irish League scoring record. By this stage they were already six points clear of the field. From then on they coasted to title number five.

Jack Vernon

The league statistics of the team since Elisha Scott took over in 1934 make just as impressive reading as those of the 1926/29 team:

Season	P	W	D	L	F	A	Pts	Pos'n
1934/35	26	17	3	6	96	36	37	3rd
1935/36	26	20	3	3	67	23	43	1st
1936/37	26	20	4	2	86	21	44	1st
1937/38	26	18	5	3	88	24	41	1st
1938/39	26	19	2	5	97	32	40	1st
1939/40	26	20	5	1	91	18	45	1st

The first to congratulate Elisha on his record-breaking achievements was the club chairman, Austin Donnelly. Between them, these two great managers had led Celtic to nine championship wins. Comparisons between the teams of Austin and Elisha were of course inevitable. But comparisons, as they say, are odious, and prove nothing. Both were great, record-breaking teams in their own right, and should be examined separately in the light of what each achieved. What can be said with certainty is that both teams, and both managers, brought nothing but glory and distinction to the name of Belfast Celtic.

Harry Walker

When you hear someone refer to the 'greatest uncapped half-back' in the history of Irish football, they are talking about Harry Walker and one of the imponderable mysteries of the time is the exclusion of this giant of the mid-field.

The son of the great John 'Jap' Walker, who played for Celtic in 1911 alongside Mickey Hamill, had spells as a youngster with Glentoran, Broadway United, Ards and Linfield before joining Celtic in 1932. In these early years, he usually played in the forward line though Walker considered himself to be a half-back. Celtic manager Jimmy McColl agreed, and for the next seventeen years, no-one ever challenged him for that position.

A brilliant defensive player, he could switch the Celtic attack into action with passes that today would be studied with the aid of a computer, and he was widely recognised as a player of unparalleled skill and ability. Walker was captain of the team during its final years and led them to victory in the explosive encounter with Scotland in New York. Prior to the game, Scotland captain George Young had commented to Walker 'I hope you can give us a bit of competition'. Harry replied 'George, I think you're in for a shock!' The Rangers centre-half has rarely had a bigger one.

Following the exit of Celtic from the League, Walker was player/manager of both Ards and Glenavon, winning the championship with the Lurgan club. He retired with medals in every competition under the jurisdiction of the Irish Football Association, and many inter-League caps. Forty years on, the question remains unanswered, 'Why was this greatest of wing-halfs never selected to play for his country?'

Hugh Kelly, Celtic goalkeeper, makes a spectacular save during the match against Linfield at Windsor Park.
Result: Celtic 4, Linfield 3.

III

The Machine Rolls On — 1940-1947

As the war situation deteriorated, the IFA decided in the summer of 1940 to suspend the Irish League and City Cup. But football went on, and Celtic participated in a new Regional League along with Linfield, Glentoran, Distillery, Cliftonville, Portadown, Glenavon and Derry City. In place of the City Cup, the clubs decided to play the Gold Cup on a league basis.

As in the pre-war years, Celtic continued to demonstrate their superiority by winning both the new competitions in their first season. The Gold Cup was a one-horse race from the first match, when Linfield were beaten 4-1. Celtic won the competition with five points to spare over their nearest rivals.

The Regional League was a marathon 28-match affair, with the teams playing each other four times. Again, Celtic were the comfortable winners, scoring 102 goals in just 27 matches (the 28th against Portadown was not played because of fixture congestion).

Of the 27 games played, one deserves special mention. On a cold January afternoon, Glenavon visited Celtic Park for what proved to be an unforgettable experience. After five minutes, their goalkeeper Hugh Kelly picked the ball out of the net after Peter O'Connor scored Celtic's first. Poor Hugh had to repeat the humiliating manoeuvre a further twelve times in the course of the afternoon, as Celtic rattled up a record-breaking 13-0 win.

The most remarkable statistic concerning this match is not that Celtic scored 13 goals, but that O'Connor helped himself to all but two of them - an individual goal-scoring record in Irish football that has still to be broken. These goals helped Peter to a total of over 70 for the season. Not bad for a makeshift centre-forward.

O'Connor scored ten less than his record in the Irish Cup Final the same year. Yet it was probably one of the most vital and pleasing of his career, as it was enough to beat Linfield.

Peter had been on target in each of the previous rounds of the Cup. He scored six in the 11-1 first-round defeat of Coleraine, and followed this by two in a 3-2 win over Bangor. In the semi-final he put two past Hugh Kelly in the Glenavon goals as Celtic won 5-2. Jimmy McAlinden scored a couple in the same match, and Artie Kelly got the fifth.

It was not one of the most memorable finals. The only goal came after 15 minutes when Harry Walker took a free kick after he had been obstructed. As the ball landed in the goal-mouth the Linfield defence hesitated. O'Connor, ever the opportunist, pounced and gave the keeper no chance with his shot.

In the second half Linfield pressed hard for the equaliser, but Tommy Breen and his defence were as resolute as they had been all season, and held out comfortably. Celtic's team for this, their third Cup victory under Elisha Scott, consisted of: Breen, McMillen and Fulton; Walker, Vernon and Leathem; Kernaghan, Kelly, O'Connor, McAlinden and McIlroy.

The following season's Regional League contained only six teams, Portadown and Glenavon having withdrawn. With the twenty matches completed, Celtic were again champions, this time with just one point to spare over Linfield. In the same season two of the team's most popular players were transferred: Jack Leathem went to Dundalk, while Tommy Breen 'defected' to Linfield.

It was also in this season that the Celtic supporters got their first look at one of the game's greatest characters. In a home league match against Derry, a 17-year-old appeared on the Celtic team at inside-left. His dazzling footwork and jinking style marked him out as one to be watched in the future. Celtic won the match 10-1, and although he didn't score, the Falls Road teenager showed glimpses of that rare genius that is granted only to a chosen few. 'Cheeky' Charlie Tully was on the threshold of a sparkling football career. Such was the strength of the Celtic panel, though, that Charlie was not to be a regular member of the team for another couple of seasons. Elisha Scott, always an astute and far-sighted manager, obviously felt that the young man needed time for his special skills to develop and mature. As a result, Tully spent a season on loan to Cliftonville and Ballyclare Comrades, and a further year in the reserves, before Elisha elevated him to his rightful position on the senior team.

For the 1942/43 season, Scott strengthened his pool with the addition of three former FAI players: Dundalk full-back Matty Cullen, Limerick's Tommy Byrne, who was the South's leading scorer, and Liam O'Neill, a clever inside-left, where he was to be a permanent fixture for the rest of the club's time in football.

Another popular signing was that of goalkeeper Hugh Kelly, the man Peter O'Connor had put eleven past just a couple of seasons earlier. Joe Douglas joined Walker and Vernon in what was to be a very settled and successful half-back line.

The team, though going through a transitional period, still managed to finish as runners-up in both the Gold Cup and Regional League. They went one better in the Cup and County Antrim Shield, winning both competitions.

Belfast Celtic, 1940/41

Celtic's second Cup Final in three years was against Glentoran; as in the previous final with Linfield, Celtic needed just one goal to lift the trophy. This came on the half-hour when Townsend picked up an O'Connor pass, and slipped the ball to outside-left Hollinger, who neatly guided it past the advancing Glentoran keeper. The Celtic team for their sixth Cup Final success consisted of: Kelly; McMillen and Fulton; Walker, Vernon and Douglas; Kernaghan, O'Connor, Byrne, Townsend and Hollinger.

Len Townsend had been signed late in the season from Brentford, and came into the team to replace the injured Paddy Bonnar. He scored four times on his debut against Cliftonville in the first round of the County Antrim Shield. He scored two more in the second round against Glentoran, and was again on target in the semi-final, as Celtic beat Bangor 5-2. Tommy Byrne picked up a hat-trick in the same match, and Harry Walker scored the other.

The final against Linfield went to two replays before Celtic emerged as 2-1 winners. Townsend scored yet again, while the Cup Final scorer Hollinger got the other. Apart from Cullen for Fulton, and McAlinden for Kernaghan, the Celtic team was the same as that which won the Cup Final.

This was Bertie Fulton's last season as a Celtic player. Apart from a short spell of academic training in London, the genial Larne man had served the club faithfully since the mid-Twenties. He had been the automatic choice at left-back for Ireland, and in his last few seasons with Celtic had captained the side with great distinction. One of the great team's unsung heroes, Bertie was content to organise the defence and encourage the less-experienced players, while allowing others to enjoy the limelight.

Celtic began the 1943/44 season by regaining the Gold Cup. They were well on their way to winning the Regional League as well, but an end-of-season fixture pile-up meant that the programme was never completed.

All rounds of the Irish Cup were completed, however, and for the third time in four years the most coveted trophy of them all found its way to the Celtic Park boardroom. As in the previous season, the first two rounds were played on a home-and-away basis. In the first round, Celtic beat Glentoran by the huge aggregate of 16-3. Distillery went down in round two to a more modest 7-1 defeat.

Tommy Byrne had already helped himself to nine goals, and fellow Southerner Liam O'Neill scored just one less. Both were on target again in the semi-final against army team ITC. Liam scored twice and Tommy once as Celtic won 3-0.

The final between Linfield and Celtic was the sixth in which the 'Big Two' were engaged. Celtic had won four of the previous five, with the Blues' only victory coming away back in 1915.

Jimmy McAlinden

Whenever memories of Belfast Celtic are exchanged, the name of Jimmy McAlinden will certainly be introduced. The brilliant inside-forward epitomized everything that the club represented in unique professionalism, total commitment and impeccable skills. Born on the Lower Falls, McAlinden was still at Milford Street School when he won three international caps on the Irish Schoolboys XI.

His first club was Glentoran where he was spotted by his namesake and Belfast Celtic Chairman, Hugh McAlinden, and brought to Celtic Park in 1934. During his career, he won medals in every competition under the jurisdiction of the Irish Intermediate and Senior Leagues, as well as winning the hearts of the supporters with his unparalleled wizardry and ball control.

In December 1938 he was transferrewd to First Division Portsmouth for a record fee of £7,500 at a time when fees of £10,000 in world football were considered a mirage. Just four months after joining the English club, he played a major role in their shock victory over League leaders Wolverhampton Wanderers in the final of the FA Cup at Wembley. The records indicate that he is the only Belfast Celtic player ever to win an English Cup medal.

On the outbreak of war, with all contracts cancelled, McAlinden returned to Celtic and, as captain, led the incomparable team of the 1940's which was virtually unbeatable. He was first choice for Ireland at inside-right in international competition, and played in all the wartime internationals which did not, unfortunately, count as 'caps'.

In 1945, he spent a season with Shamrock Rovers before returning to Portsmouth, and two years later transferred to Stoke City and later Southend United. As a manager, he achieved even greater prominence. His thirteen-year reign with Glenavon brought the Lurgan club every trophy in the IFA cupboard and with Distillery, he took the Whites into Europe for the first and only time on their history. His football career ended with the management of Drogheda in the FAI League. Few Irish footballers have ever equalled the heights scaled by this great Belfast Celtic player.

Belfast Celtic, 1944

Back Row *(left to right): H. Walker, W. McMillan, H. Kelly, J. Vernon, J. Douglas, M. Cullen.*
Front Row: *P. O'Connor, C. Tully, J. McAlinden, P. Bonnar, C. Currie.*

Liam O'Neill

Linfield's hopes of breaking their rivals' winning sequence were dented after only 15 minutes, when Celtic captain Jimmy McAlinden pushed a Billy Collins cross into the path of Paddy Bonnar, who made no mistake. Collins was playing only his second senior game, coming on at outside-right for the injured Kernaghan.

If the Windsor team's hopes were dented then, they were well and truly dashed just 12 minutes later when McAlinden scored the second himself. To complete a miserable day for the Linfield supporters Artie Kelly drove through a third after picking up a pass from man-of-the-match McAlinden. A late Cochrane goal was little consolation for the Blues, as they lost 3-1. Celtic's winning line-up was H. Kelly; McMillen and Cullen; Walker, Vernon and O'Connor; Collins, McAlinden, Byrne, A. Kelly and Bonnar. To make things worse for the Blues, it was in this same season that Celtic inflicted their biggest-ever defeat on them - a massive 8-1 drubbing in the County Antrim Shield. Kernaghan and O'Neill each scored a hat-trick.

In the next two seasons, Celtic were runners-up in the Regional League. It was fitting that they should win the County Antrim Shield in 1945, exactly 50 years after they first won the trophy in the days when they were still playing junior football.

After a goal-less draw with Linfield in the final, Celtic won the replay by virtue of a typical Jimmy McAlinden goal, when he beat two defenders before stroking the ball past Tommy Breen in the Linfield goals. This was Jimmy's last goal for Celtic. In the close season, he moved south to play for Shamrock Rovers.

Charlie Tully's inclusion in the team was one of the brightest aspects of the season. With his brilliant footwork, perfect ball-control and precision passing, he set up many goal-scoring chances for his grateful team-mates. Even at this early stage, Charlie was already being described as the cleverest forward in the Irish League.

Elisha Scott was always on the look-out for new talent to keep Celtic at the top. Two promising right-sided players, Johnny Campbell and Johnny Denver, had been brought to Celtic Park in 1944/45. To these Elisha added a pair of centre-forwards with reputations for scoring goals - Corkman Sean McCarthy and Eddie McMorran from Larne.

The new forward line of Denver or Campbell, Tully, McCarthy or McMorran, O'Neill and Bonnar helped Celtic win the Gold Cup in 1945/46. They won nine of their games, scoring 30 goals and conceding only 10. McCarthy was top scorer with 13. He picked up a couple in his debut against Glentoran, and continued to score at the rate of a goal a game.

Although the War was now over, the Irish league did not resume in the 1946/47 season. Ballymena and Coleraine were added to the Regional league, to bring the number back up to eight. This increase in membership was accompanied by Celtic's third championship win in the six years in which the programme was completed.

The Celtic team was now as strong and balanced as it had ever been. With Hugh Kelly going into temporary retirement, Kevin McAlinden returned as first-choice goalkeeper. Billy McMillen was partnered at full-back by the impressive ex-Limerick player Tom 'Bud' Aherne, whose sterling play at left-back earned him his first cap against England, along with Joe Douglas, Jack Vernon and Eddie McMorran.

The Walker-Vernon-Douglas half-back line was broken when Jack moved to West Bromwich Albion in mid-season. His absence created no problem, however, as Charlie Currie, who had been signed some time earlier from Cliftonville, stepped in to admirably fill the gap. While the defence was keeping opposing forwards at bay, the Celtic attack was delighting the supporters with goals galore. Centre-forward Eddie McMorran scored 31 goals out of a total of 95. These included double hat-tricks against both Coleraine and Ballymena. Campbell and Denver combined well on the right wing, while O'Neill and Bonnar served up some delightful football on the left.

Celtic won the League at a canter, and looked forward to picking up a League/Cup double. The hero of the cup final was a man who, regrettably, had not taken much in the winning of the league.

Charlie Tully had been carried off injured in only the fifth league game of the season. A combination of this injury and a bout of glandular fever kept him out of football for a few months.

Just a couple of weeks before his injury, Charlie's potential had been noticed by Mr S. Seymour, a Newcastle United representative. Mr Seymour had attended a Linfield/Celtic match to gauge the performance of a Linfield player. But it was 'Cheeky Charlie' who caught his eye as he engineered a 2-0 Celtic win. 'Clever little fellow, that Tully chap,' said the Englishman, 'he should be in international class shortly.' How right he was.

Charlie was fully fit for the Cup Final against Glentoran. Celtic were under pressure in the first half, but Kevin McAlinden and his defence reacted confidently, and kept the score down to 0-0 at half-time.

The second-half was only seven minutes old when two Glentoran defenders hesitated over a loose ball. While they were waiting for each other to make a move, Tully nipped in between them, left them flat-footed, and beat the keeper

Eddie McMorran

Charlie Currie

Bud Aherne

John Denver

with a well-placed, left-footed shot. This piece of sheer opportunism was enough to win the cup for Celtic.

This was Celtic's eighth and last Cup win in 12 Finals. The team line-up: McAlinden, McMillen and Aherne; Walker, Currie and Lawlor; Campbell, Tully, McMorran, Denver and Douglas.

Robin Lawlor came into the team due to the absence of the unfortunate Paddy Bonnar, who missed his second Cup Final through injury. Joe Douglas moved up to outside-left, leaving the wing-half position open for Robin.

Before winning the 'double', Celtic had already regained the Gold Cup, scoring 52 goals and conceding only 12 in 14 games. Half-way through the programme they inflicted a 9-0 defeat on Glentoran - the worst result in that club's long history. The quick-witted Celtic supporters, always ready to take advantage of their opponents' discomfort, soon came up with a new phrase, 'Nine times around the Glens for a bob.'

As in the league, Eddie McMorran was the top scorer with 20 goals. Eddie's exploits had not gone unnoticed 'across the water'. At the end of the season he was signed by Manchester City.

Manager Scott did not lose any sleep over the Larne man's departure - he knew there was no need to look for a replacement, he already had one of Ireland's best centre-forwards on the playing staff. Elisha had been in football long enough to recognise that this 19-year-old had the potential to be one of the best-ever centre-forwards. Jimmy Jones had already demonstrated his facility for scoring goals in a friendly with Glasgow Celtic. A large crowd watched in admiration as the reserve striker scored a hat-trick in a thrilling 4-4 draw. In the next season and a half, Jimmy was to fully justify his manager's faith in him.

Robin Lawlor, Belfast Celtic left-half, in action

Belfast Celtic, 1946/47

Manager Elisha Scott instructs the team

IV

A Historic Season — 1947-1948

A Belfast Celtic team of 1895 won a Senior trophy while still in the Junior ranks; the 1918 team won the Irish Cup while playing in the Intermediate League; Austin Donnelly's Twenties team twice went through the League undefeated; Elisha Scott's team of the Thirties won five League titles in a row; the 1940 team was undefeated in 36 successive matches; the War team won three Regional Leagues and four IFA Cups. And yet one of the most glorious chapters in the history of the club was still to be written.

The Celtic team of 1947/48 not only picked up a trio of trophies in the League, City Cup and Gold Cup - they did it with a dominance which has never been rivalled. Indeed, from the end of August until the following March, Elisha's team were not only undefeated, but actually WON a magnificent 31 successive matches. At the beginning of this record run, goalkeeper Hugh Kelly, who had returned to the team after a year's absence, did not concede a single goal in nine matches in a row.

The City Cup had last been competed for in the 1939/40 season. Celtic had won it then, and were now to retain it in magnificent style. A look at the statistics illustrates the superiority of Celtic in this competition:

P	W	D	L	F	A	Pts
11	10	0	1	36	7	20

The paltry 'goals against' figure demonstrates the solidity of the great Celtic defence. Keeper Kelly chalked up no less than eight clean sheets in the 11-match programme. Hugh was undoubtedly delighted to be playing behind such accomplished and uncompromising defenders as Billy McMillen, Bud Aherne, Harry Walker, Charlie Currie, Joe Douglas and Robin Lawlor. This must rate as one of the most formidable defensive lines that the Irish League has ever seen.

And of course the forwards played their part, scoring at the rate of more than three a game. A look at the line-up would have been enough to strike terror into the hearts of even the stoutest defenders: John Denver, Johnny Campbell, Jimmy Jones, Charlie Tully or Liam O'Neill, Paddy Bonnar. Each of these was an immensely gifted individual in his own right - put together, they were quite simply irresistible.

"Read the 'Ulster', Harry"

The match between Celtic and Linfield at Celtic park had been hard fought and there were groans from the supporters on the Willowbank Hill as referee Tommy Hunter awarded a goal to Linfield from what looked suspiciously like an offside position. The Celtic captain, Harry Walker, immediately protested - 'Referee! That was no goal!' Hunter replied "Was it not? Read the 'Ulster' tonight, Harry."

The one game that Celtic lost in the City Cup was to Bangor at the end of August. From then until mid-March, they won every match they played. This record of 31 successive victories is one that still stands over 40 years later.

Like the City Cup, the Irish League also resumed in this season. Needless to say, with Celtic in such devastating form, they ended up as League Champions. They thus extended their own record of successive championships to six - a record which also remains unbroken.

They started off the League in whirlwind style, scoring at the rate of five a game for the first half-dozen matches. In the first match, Ards were on the receiving end of a fine Charlie Tully hat-trick. Johnny Campbell and Jimmy Jones were on target in the same match.

The form of Jones in particular was a revelation. Jimmy was one of that rare breed of centre-forward whose only thought on receiving the ball is to bury it in the back of the net. His goal against Ards was followed by a hat-trick against Portadown and four against a hapless Coleraine side which went down 8-1. In fact, Jimmy's name was an almost permanent feature on the score-sheet right throughout the League campaign. He totalled 28 goals in 22 games, to add to the 15 that had helped his team to retain the City Cup.

Of course, Celtic didn't rely on Jones alone to provide the all-important goals. Both Johnny Campbell and Liam O'Neill were in tremendous form all season. They contributed 40 goals between them in the League and City Cup. And the wizardry of the two wingers, John Denver on the right and Paddy Bonnar on the left, continued to bemuse the opposition and delight their supporters.

Paddy's cup jinx struck again this season, however, as he was injured for the Gold Cup Final against Distillery. Johnny Campbell was also unfit, and his place was taken by talented reserve winger Jack Robinson. With only 15 minutes gone, the Final was over as a contest. A Billy McMillen free kick after five minutes put Celtic one up (the forwards didn't have a monopoly on goal-scoring). A second was soon added by the consistent Liam O'Neill. The 2-0 success gave Celtic their third consecutive Gold Cup victory.

To underline their superiority, Celtic rounded off this historic season by showing that they had no equals throughout Ireland. In the early rounds of the North/South Tournament, they disposed of League of Ireland teams Drumcondra and Limerick. A 4-2 aggregate victory over FAI Cup winners Shamrock Rovers in the semi-final put them into the final against Distillery. A 2-1 win over the Whites - Paddy Bonnar scored both goals - gave Celtic the unofficial title of 'All-Ireland Champions'.

Billy McMillen

"Give it to me, Paddy!"

It happened during a match at Celtic Park as Paddy Bonnar was working his way through the opposing defence. At inside left, Charlie Tully, unmarked, quickly sized up the opportunity and shouted "Give it to me, Paddy". Bonnar stopped, bent down and picked up the ball in his hands and gave it to a bewildered Tully with the words "OK, Charlie, you wanted the ball - There it is!" The crowd roared. Scott probably went into convulsions and the referee could only say "Dammit, Paddy, that's a handball."

Charlie Tully

Forget Pele, Best, Maradonna and the rest. For sheer footballing genius, breath-taking skills and delightful unpredictability, Charles Patrick Tully can have few equals. The Falls Road-born man displayed his prodigious talents to enraptured Belfast Celtic supporters during the 1940's. At the end of the 1946/47 season, he was snapped up by Glasgow Celtic manager Jimmy McGrory for £8,000.

The 'Clown Prince of Football' immediately set about transforming the fortunes of that great club. Overnight, he became the idol of the Celtic fans when he was instrumental in a 3-1 defeat of Rangers in the League Cup.

Throughout the 50's, Charlie was the undisputed star of Scottish football. His career reached its zenith in 1957, when he was in the team which trounced Rangers 7-1 in the League Cup Final - a result which is still commemorated on the walls of Glasgow!

Yet throughout these glory days, Charlie never forgot the other Celtic, where it all began. Like everyone else, he was shocked to learn of the Belfast's club withdrawal from football. He also hoped that Belfast Celtic would return one day, and recorded his willingness to be part of any new set-up.

When Charlie left Glasgow, there was still no Belfast Celtic. He spent a spell with FAI club Cork Hibs, before returning North as manager of Bangor and Portadown. When he died in 1971, the Falls Road came to a virtual standstill for his funeral. He will always live in the memories of those who witnessed his football genius.

Charlie Tully had a mixed year. A recurrence of his glandular trouble in early January put him out of the team until mid-March. But when he did play, Charlie enraptured the Celtic supporters with his extraordinary talent and flamboyant character. And he certainly did enough to impress the representatives of Glasgow Celtic, who paid out £8,000 in June to bring him to the Scottish 'Paradise'.

Charlie immediately became a big hit with the Glasgow fans, and established a reputation as the 'Clown Prince of Football'. He was also to play ten times for Ireland, his most memorable game being in a 2-2 draw with England at Windsor park. Charlie scored both the home team's goals in this match, one of them direct from a corner kick.

Paddy Bonnar

Paddy Bonnar belonged to that particular school of players who believed that football should be entertainment, and few achieved his popularity and adulation. His 'foot over the ball' trick was as predictable as the sunrise but it continued to confuse the opposing defenders and delight the crowds. And when Bonnar pulled the ball over to his left foot from twenty-five yards out, the crowds expected, and usually got, a rocketing drive that whistled like a World War I shell.

Paddy Bonnar was born in Ballymena, but came to Belfast at an early age where he learned his football with the local youngsters in the Bog Meadows. His early clubs included Distillery and St James Gate of the FAI League before joining Celtic in the 1941/42 season. He received international honours three times during the Victory wartime encounters, and was first choice in the outside-left position on the inter-league teams. During the ill-fated Boxing Day encounter with Linfield in 1948, Bonnar had the good fortune to be sent off during the match. Had he not, he would have been trapped at the Railway end during the pitch invasion with results that cannot be contemplated.

He toured with Belfast Celtic in North America, then transferred to second division Barnsley, where he teamed up with another Belfast great, Danny Blanchflower. Other clubs included Aldershot, Ballymena United and Derry City. It is a tribute to his fitness and endurance that he was still playing brilliant attacking football at the age of 38.

Paddy Bonnar will be remembered particularly for a philosophy that packed football grounds and delighted supporters - 'Get the ball and put it in the net'. It would seem that many football administrators today do not understand that.

Record 31 Successive Wins - 1947/48

	Competition	Opposition	Score	Scorer(s)
1.	Gold Cup	Coleraine (H)	5-0	Denvir 2, Tully, Bonnar, McMillen
2.	City Cup	Cliftonville (H)	3-0	Jones, Robinson, Denver
3.	Gold Cup(semi-F)	Glentoran (H)	1-0	O'Neill
4.	City Cup	Distillery (H)	2-0	Jones, O'Neill
5.	Gold Cup (Final)	Distillery (Solitude)	2-0	McMillen, O'Neill
6.	City Cup	Derry City (A)	7-0	Jones 2, O'Neill 2, Denver 2, Tully
7.	City Cup	Glenavon (A)	3-0	O'Neill, Jones 2
8.	City Cup	Ballymena (H)	4-0	Jones 3, Campbell
9.	City Cup	Portadown (A)	4-0	O'Neill 2, Jones, Campbell
10.	City Cup	Linfield (A)	4-3	O'Neill 2, Jones, Tully
11.	City Cup	Coleraine (H)	3-1	Campbell 2, Bonnar
12.	Irish League	Ards (H)	5-2	Tully 3, Campbell, Jones
13.	Irish League	Portadown (H)	6-2	Jones 3, Denver, O'Neill, Bonnar
14.	Irish League	Distillery (A)	2-0	Jones, O'Neill
15.	Irish League	Coleraine (A)	8-1	O'Neill 2, Jones 4, Campbell, Bonnar
16.	Irish League	Cliftonville (H)	3-0	O'Neill, Jones, Denver
17.	Irish League	Derry City (A)	5-1	O'Neill 2, Campbell 2, Bonnar
18.	Irish League	Glenavon (H)	3-1	Campbell, Jones 2
19.	Irish League	Glentoran (A)	3-1	Jones 2, O'Neill
20.	Irish League	Linfield (H)	3-0	Jones, Campbell 2
21.	Irish League	Bangor (A)	5-2	Jones 2, Tully, O'Neill, Denver
22.	Irish League	Ballymena (H)	2-0	Jones, O'Neill
23.	Irish League	Ards (H)	6-0	Jones 3, O'Neill, Denver, Montgomery
24.	Irish League	Portadown (A)	4-1	O'Neill, Denver 2, Bonnar
25.	Irish Cup R1	Cliftonville (H)	2-0	Jones 2
26.	Irish League	Distillery (H)	5-0	Bonnar, O'Neill 2, Campbell 2
27.	Irish League	Coleraine (H)	5-2	Campbell 3, Jones, o.g.
28.	Irish Cup R2	Brantwood (H)	4-0	Jones 2, Bonnar, Denver
29.	Irish League	Cliftonville (A)	4-2	McGarry, Tucker, Jones, o.g.
30.	Irish League	Derry City (H)	5-1	McGarry, Campbell, Jones 2, Bonnar
31.	Irish League	Glenavon (A)	3-1	Campbell 2, Bonnar
	Goal Total		**121 - 21**	

Belfast Celtic, 1948/49

Back row (left to right): *McGuigan (Trainer), Lawlor, O'Neill, McMillen, McAlinden, Currie, Aherne, Scott (Manager).*
Front row: Campbell, Haslett, Jones, Walker (Captain), Bonnar, Davis, Douglas.

V

The Jimmy Jones Incident — 1948-1949

Although they started the new season without the services of Charlie Tully, the champions were nevertheless in an optimistic mood. Little did they realise in August that this was to be their last year in football. All the club's dreams and aspirations, all their hopes for further glory, were to be shattered in one shameful December afternoon.

The season had started in a very satisfactory manner. In their eleven City Cup games, Celtic remained undefeated, taking the trophy with 20 points. As in the season before, Jimmy Jones was the hero in the unbeaten run. In spite of missing a couple of matches due to a fractured jaw which he sustained against Glentoran, Jimmy still managed to score 15 goals in 9 games. These included hat-tricks against Derry, Cliftonville and Glenavon.

This great centre-forward began the League campaign in equally irresistible form. In the seven matches up to Boxing Day, he added another dozen goals to his tally. Observers were confidently predicting that he would beat his previous season's record of 61 goals. No-one, however, could have predicted the terrible events which would almost end his football career.

The atmosphere was intense at Windsor park on the afternoon of Boxing Day, 1948. Everyone in the 25,000 crowd knew what was at stake. A win for Celtic would bring them within one point of the leaders Linfield. A win for the Blues would virtually ensure that the League Championship trophy ended up at Windsor.

The match itself was a tough, uncompromising affair. Before the interval, Linfield's Bryson was carried off injured after an accidental collision with Jones. A half-time announcement over the public address system that Bryson had sustained a broken leg further aggravated an already volatile situation.

In the second half, Linfield's Currie and Paddy Bonnar of Celtic were ordered off the pitch for fighting. Then, ten minutes from the end, Johnny Denver was pulled down in the penalty area. Captain Harry Walker assumed the responsibility of taking the penalty, and calmly put the ball out of goalkeeper Russell's reach to score the first goal of the match. The lead was short-lived.

Just three minutes later, Simpson scored the equaliser, and the game ended in a 1-1 draw.

It was not so much what happened on the field of play, but the sickening incidents after the final whistle had blown, that made this day one of the blackest in the history of Irish sport. Although Linfield had maintained their lead at the top of the table, a section of their supporters had made up their minds that they wanted blood. What was to occur next was to bring shame and disgrace on the name of the great club which they professed to support.

As the Celtic players were leaving the pitch on their way to the pavilion, they were mercilessly attacked by a section of the crowd and had to literally run for their lives. During his anxious attempt to escape, the unfortunate Jimmy Jones, who seemed to be a particular target, was pushed over a parapet on to the terracing. Here he was set upon so savagely that it was feared that he would never kick a ball again. He suffered multiple bruises, had his leg broken, and had to be carried in an unconscious state to the dressing room.

Jimmy was not the only victim of the mob. Robin Lawlor and Kevin McAlinden were also injured on their retreat form the pitch. Kevin received such a manhandling in fact that he was out of the team for the next two months.

All decent-thinking people were shattered by the incident. The Linfield directors published a statement expressing their regret, while all the true Linfield supporters also made their own feelings of disgust known through letters to the press.

The Celtic directors were understandably appalled by the treatment meted out to their players. In a strongly-worded statement, they protested against 'the conduct of those responsible for the protection of the players in failing to take measures either to prevent the brutal attack or to deal with it with any degree of effectiveness after it developed.'

But the directors went further than merely lodge a protest. Although it was not reported at the time, they decided at the same meeting that Belfast Celtic Football Club would withdraw from football. Only be doing this could they be certain that such a ghastly occurrence would never be repeated.

In the meantime, Celtic continued to fulfil their fixtures until the end of the season. Johnny Campbell moved to the centre-forward position vacated by Jones. And he must have borrowed Jimmy's boots, because his name appeared regularly on the score sheet for the next couple of months. He notched up no less than six in a single game against Distillery, just a couple of weeks after the Windsor fiasco. Celtic won that particular match 10-2, with 8 of the goals coming in the first half.

Jimmy Jones

If there was one position in the football structure that Belfast Celtic made their own, it must be that of centre forward. Names like Sammy Curran, Davy 'Boy' Martin, Peter O'Connor, Jimmy Turnbull and Eddie McMorran are forever engraved in the minds of those who have a special admiration for those who today we term 'the striker'. To this illustrious role must be added the name of Jimmy Jones.

The first love of the Keady-born centre forward was cricket, which he played with Waringstown Boys. He began playing soccer while still at school with Lurgan Tech and the Boys Brigade, followed by spells with the Lurgan Intermediate club Sunnyside and Glenavon Juniors. Introduced to Linfield by his cousin Jack Jones, the famed Linfield captain, the youngster was thrown into a trial match composed of Linfield players and ended the day by scoring three goals. Incredibly the Blues failed to retain him.

It was a mistake that would not only cost them dearly, but would arguably change the face of Irish football. He returned to Lurgan to play with the local amateur team, Shankill Young Men, where he scored six goals in a cup match against Hilden Rec.

Watching the game from the sidelines was Elisha Scott, and the Celtic manager's powers of persuasion brought Jones to Paradise in the middle of the 1946/47 season. In his first full season with Belfast Celtic, Jones scored 63 goals and by half-way through the ill-fated 1948/49 season, he had already reached 33 goals when the infamous Boxing Day incident at Windsor Park put the brakes on a career that was headed for the heights.

By the time he had recovered, Celtic were out of football and Jones signed for Glenavon where he continued his exceptional career, with 74 goals in one season and an average of 50 in the others. Jones won three international caps and several league caps, and participated in the U.S. tour with Glenavon where he ended his playing career.

The Lurgan man remains today as one of the most popular players ever to wear the green and white. His fearless atacks and spirited competitiveness will long be remembered by Celtic fans everywhere.

Another big win came a few weeks later against Derry City, when the Brandywell team received an 8-0 drubbing. Campbell again scored a couple, but the hero of the match was George Silcock, a recent signing from Glenavon, who scored 5 goals.

But despite these and other convincing victories, and despite such promising players including ex-Antrim Gaelic football star Harry O'Neill, the fall-out from the notorious Boxing Day match continued to be felt. The general feeling was that Irish football could never be quite the same.

The actual decision to withdraw was not made public knowledge until the eve of the American tour in late April, but astute observers were already reading the signs. In early March, Johnny Campbell and Robin Lawlor were transferred to Fulham. This was closely followed by 'Bud' Aherne's departure for Luton, and an arrangement between Celtic and Barnsley for the transfer of Paddy Bonnar. Slowly but surely it was beginning to dawn on the club's shocked supporters that the entire team was up for sale.

The supporters' worst fears were realised when, on April 21st 1949, it was reported that Celtic had written to the Irish Football League requesting permission to withdraw from membership. The permission was granted, and Crusaders were admitted to the League in Celtic's place.

Just one week later, the Celtic players and officials set off for America in what was to be the last-ever series of matches in the great club's 60-year history.

94

Jimmy Jones, Belfast Celtic centre forward, in action.

Johnny Campbell

The Derry-born outside right was discovered by the Belfast Celtic trainer Paddy McGuigan in the mid 1940's as the successor to Norman Kernaghan, and quickly established himself as a winger of outstanding ability.

During his teenage years, Campbell had developed an interest in athletics and at one time had held both the 100 and 200 yards Ulster sprint championships. A former cattle-drover, Campbell must have felt completely at home as he sent the defensive herds of opposing teams blundering around in circles. His tremendous speed and opportunism added a deadly mixture to a forward line which included Charlie Tully, Jackie Denver, Jimmy Jones and Paddy Bonar.

The name of Johnny Campbell has a place in the history books because of his incredible achievement against the Scottish international side during the Celtic tour of North America. On May 29th 1949 at the Triborough Stadium in New York, he scored both goals in the Belfast club's shock victory over the British champions.

When the club retired from football, Campbell was transferred to Fulham along with team-mate Robin Lawlor, and served his new team faithfully until forced to end his career through ill health. On his return to Belfast, he continued as a scout for the London club until his untimely death in January 1968 at the age of 44.

SAVAGE ATTACK ON CELTIC PLAYERS AT WINDSOR
Vigorous Protest by Celtic Directors

THE OUTRAGEOUS ATTACK ON THE CELTIC TEAM WHEN LEAVING THE PLAYING PITCH ON THEIR WAY TO THE PAVILION AT THE CONCLUSION OF THE IRISH LEAGUE MATCH v. LINFIELD AT WINDSOR PARK COMPELS THE CELTIC DIRECTORS, IN THE INTERESTS OF THEIR PLAYERS, SUPPORTERS, AND FOOTBALL IN GENERAL, TO ISSUE THE FOLLOWING STATEMENT:—

"The attack, the directors feel, in its gravity is without parallel in the annals of football. In the course of it the players were thrown to the ground and kicked. Jimmy Jones, the Celtic centre-forward, received multiple injuries, including a broken leg, which may totally incapacitate him from football.

"During the whole of this concerted attack, the protection afforded to the unfortunate players may be fairly described as quite inadequate.

"In the circumstances, the directors wish to make the strongest possible protest against the conduct of those responsible for the protection of the players in failing to take measures either to prevent the brutal attack or to deal with it with any degree of effectiveness after it developed."

Epilogue

Belfast Celtic never played football again after their American trip, apart from a couple of exhibition matches for charity. For years the club's faithful supporters continued to hope against hope that the directors would have a change of heart. In an exhibition match against Glasgow Celtic in 1952, which attracted a crowd of almost 30,000, a large banner on the terracing contained the plea which was in everyone's heart: 'Will ye no come back again?'

We know now the answer to that question. Belfast Celtic will not be back. The Donegall Road stadium no longer exists. Everything was flattened and cleared to make way for yet another shopping centre.

Yet although the last tangible association with Celtic has gone, the name lives on in the folklore of West Belfast. When sports fans gather to discuss the 'Golden Age' of Irish Football, you can always be sure of one thing:

THE BELFAST CELTIC WILL BE THERE.

*

Many people would argue that the notorious 'Boxing Day Incident' was not the real reason for Celtic's departure from football. Among other things it has been rumoured that there was a major rift within the Board which couldn't be healed. But there is no firm evidence to support such rumours. I cannot believe that the fine people who comprised the Belfast Celtic Board of Directors would put personal differences or financial considerations above the very existence of the great team which they were proud and privileged to represent. Surely they would not have deprived the sport-loving people of West Belfast (and further afield) of the pleasure of watching their idols, if they could have found any alternative solution to complete withdrawal from football?

The sad fact of the matter is that the Belfast of the late Forties was no different from that of the early Twenties or the Eighties. The rivalry between Belfast Celtic and Linfield was simply too intense to be healthy. A match between the two teams always held the potential for serious spectator violence. The only way to remove the threat was for one of the teams to withdraw from the Irish League. Sadly, from the point of view of their supporters, it was the Celtic Board which took the unpalatable but necessary decision. By doing so, they undoubtedly saved an untold number of people from being seriously injured.

Joint Captains, Clarlie Tully (left), Glasgow Celtic, and Jack Vernon, Belfast Celtic.
Exhibition match, 1952, Celtic Park.

Norman Kernaghan, Harry Walker, Jack Vernon and Charlie Tully return to 'Paradise'.

The Boardroom in later years. Harry Walker, Jack Vernon and Charlie Tully with the Charity Cup.

Statistical Appendixes

1

Belfast Celtic's Record in all Competitions

Irish League Champions (14)
1900, 1915, 1920, 1926, 1927, 1928, 1929, 1933, 1936, 1937, 1938, 1939, 1940, 1948.

Irish League Runners-Up (4)
1905, 1909, 1934, 1949.

Belfast & District League Champions (once) 1919.

Regional League Champions (3)
1941, 1942, 1947.

Regional League Runners-Up (3)
1943, 1945, 1946.

Irish Cup Winners (8)
1918, 1926, 1937, 1938, 1941, 1943, 1944, 1947.

Irish Cup Runners-Up (4)
1906, 1915, 1917, 1929.

City Cup Winners (11)
1906, 1907, 1919, 1926, 1928, 1930, 1931, 1933, 1940, 1948, 1949.

City Cup Runners-Up (8)
1902, 1903, 1911, 1920, 1927, 1932, 1934, 1935

Gold Cup Winners (10)
1912, 1926, 1935, 1939, 1940, 1941, 1944, 1946, 1947, 1948.

Gold Cup Runners-Up (4)
1928, 1931, 1938, 1943.

County Antrim Shield Winners (8)
1895, 1910, 1927, 1936, 1937, 1939, 1943, 1945

County Antrim Shield Runners-Up (9)
1893, 1894, 1904, 1919, 1920, 1925, 1932, 1933, 1944.

League and Cup Doubles (3)
1926, 1937, 1938

2

(a) Belfast Celtic's Irish League Record

Season	Plyd	W	D	L	F	A	Pts	Place
1896/97	10	1	2	7	11	25	4	6th
1897/98	10	3	1	6	15	19	7	4th
1898/99	10	2	2	6	15	25	6	5th
1899/00	8	5	1	2	18	11	11	1st
1900/01	10	4	2	4	13	13	10	3rd
1901/02	14	4	4	6	22	25	12	5th
1902/03	14	7	2	5	35	23	16	4th
1903/04	14	5	2	7	27	20	12	4th
1904/05	14	9	3	2	21	10	21	2nd
1905/06	14	6	3	5	20	18	15	4th
1906/07	14	4	3	7	18	25	11	6th
1907/08	13	5	1	7	20	20	11	6th
1908/09	14	5	2	7	26	33	12	6th
1909/10	14	9	0	5	25	13	18	2nd
1910/11	14	5	5	4	21	19	15	3rd
1911/12	14	7	6	1	21	11	20	3rd
1912/13	18	7	4	7	24	26	18	6th
1913/14	14	8	1	5	19	18	17	3rd
1914/15	14	10	3	1	24	7	23	1st
1919/20	14	10	3	1	27	6	23	1st
1924/25	22	11	5	6	36	31	27	3rd
1925/26	22	16	1	5	52	38	33	1st
1926/27	22	15	7	0	66	36	37	1st
1927/28	26	20	5	1	101	35	45	1st
1928/29	26	22	4	0	116	23	48	1st
1929/30	26	13	4	9	68	57	30	4th
1930/31	26	16	4	6	75	52	36	3rd
1931/32	26	14	5	7	55	36	33	3rd
1932/33	26	19	3	4	81	34	41	1st
1933/34	26	17	3	6	74	41	37	2nd
1934/35	26	17	3	6	96	35	37	3rd
1935/36	26	20	3	3	67	23	43	1st
1936/37	26	20	4	2	86	21	44	1st
1937/38	26	18	5	3	88	24	41	1st
1938/39	26	19	2	5	97	32	40	1st
1939/40	26	20	5	1	91	18	45	1st
1947/48	22	19	1	2	84	26	39	1st
1948/49	22	14	3	5	69	32	31	2nd

(b) Belfast and District League Record

Season	Plyd	W	D	L	F	A	Pts	Place
1918/19	10	7	1	2	15	7	15	1st

(c) Regional League Record

1040/41	27	19	4	4	104	32	42	1st
1941/42	20	12	6	2	57	23	30	1st
1942/43	20	13	3	4	50	22	29	2nd
1944/45	20	13	5	2	57	27	31	2nd
1945/46	20	14	4	2	58	20	32	2nd
1946/47	28	21	2	5	96	41	44	1st

3

Managers' League Records

Name	Played	W	D	L	C'ships won
Jimmie Blessington 1913/14	14	8	1	5	-
Jimmy Magowan 1914/15	14	10	3	1	1
Austin Donnelly 1915/20 1924/29	132	94	25	13	5
Archie Heggarty 1929/32	78	43	13	22	-
Jimmy McColl 1932/34	52	36	6	10	1
Elisha Scott 1934/49	200	147	26	27	6

4

'Victory' Internationalists

1919

Hamill, M.	(2)
Kerr, E.	(1)
McKinney, D.	(2)

1946

Aherne, T.	(2)
Bonnar, P.	(2)
McCarthy, S.	(1)
McMillan, W.	(3)
Vernon, J.	(3)

Note: 'Victory' Internationals were played in celebration after the ending of war.

5.

Belfast Celtic's Record in Irish Cup Finals

1906 Shelbourne 2 Celtic 0
Team: Haddock; McClelland, Pinkerton, Maxwell, Connor, Nicholl; Gall, Mulholland, Runnigan, Maguire, Devlin.

1915 Linfield 1 Celtic 0
Team: Mehaffey; Nelson, Barrett; Leathem, Hamill, Norwood; Kerr, McKnight, Williams, Marshall, Cowell.

1917 Glentoran 2 Celtic 0
Team: Scott; Kennedy, McIlroy; Norwood, Hamill, Stewart; McKinney, Kelly, Heaney, Johnston, Frazer.

1918 Celtic 2 Linfield 0 (Stewart 2)
Team: Scott; McStay, Barrett; Mulligan, Hamill, Stewart; McKinney, McIlroy, Ferris, Johnston, Frazer.

1926 Celtic 3 Linfield 2 (Curran 3)
Team: Fitzmaurice; Scott, Ferguson; Pollock, Moore, Perry; McGrillen, Ferris, Curran, S. Mahood, J. Mahood.

1929 Ballymena 2 Celtic 1 (J. Mahood)
Team: Diffen; Wallace, Fulton; Moore, Hamill, Pollock; Gallagher, Ferris, Curran, S. Mahood, J. Mahood.

1937 Celtic 3 Linfield 0 (Turnbull 3)
Team: McAlinden; McMillen, Lavery; H. Walker, Leathem, J. Walker; Kernaghan, McArdle, Turnbull, Bruce, McIlroy.

1938 Celtic 2 Bangor 1 (McAlinden, Bruce)
Team: K. McAlinden; Lavery, Fulton; H. Walker, Leathem, J. Walker; Kernaghan, J. McAlinden, Kelly, Bruce, McIlroy.

1941 Celtic 1 Linfield 0 (O'Connor)
Team: Breen; McMillen, Fulton; Walker, Vernon, Leathem; Kernaghan, Kelly, O'Connor, McAlinden, McIlroy.

1943 Celtic 1 Glentoran 0 (Hollinger)
Team: Kelly; McMillen, Fulton; Walker, Vernon, Douglas; Kernaghan, O'Connor, Byrne, Townsend, Hollinger.

1944 Celtic 3 Linfield 1 (Bonnar, McAlinden, Kelly)
Team: H. Kelly; McMillen, Cullen; Walker, Vernon, O'Connor; Collins, McAlinden, Byrne, A Kelly, Bonnar.

1947 Celtic 1 Glentoran 0 (Tully)
Team: McAlinden; McMillen, Aherne; Walker, Currie, Lawlor; Campbell, Tully, McMorran, Denver, Douglas.

6

Irish International Appearances

Name	First Cap	(With Celtic)	Total Caps
Aherne, T.	1947		4
Breen, T.	1935		9
Clarke, R.	1901		2
Connor, J.	1901	(1905)	13
Coulter, J.	1934		11
Curran, S.	1926		3
Diffen, J.	1931		1
Doherty, I.	1901		1
Douglas, J.P.	1947		1
Ferris, J.	1920		5
Fulton, R.P.	1930		20
Hamill, M.	1912	(1920)	7
Hunter, A.	1905	(1908)	8
Kernaghan, N.	1936		3
Leathem, J.	1939		1
McAlinden, J.	1938		4
McAuley, P.	1900		1
McCann, P.	1910		7
McCullough, K.	1935		5
McGrillen, J.	1924	(1927)	2
McKee, F.W.	1906	(1914)	5
McMorran, E.J.	1947		15
Macartney, A.	1903	(1907)	15
Mahood, J.	1926		9
Martin, D.K.	1934		10
Maxwell, J.	1902	(1906)	7
Mulholland, S.	1906'		2
Nicholl, H	1902		3
Scott, E.	1920	(1935)	31
Vernon, J.	1947		17

Players like Charlie Tully, who did not win any caps as a Belfast Celtic player, are not included.

7

Transfers to Cross-Channel Clubs

Date	Player	Transferred To
1903	W. Clay	Sheffield United
1909	P. Warren	Sheffield United
1909	P. O'Connell	Sheffield United
1909	A. Hunter	Sheffield United
1910	M. Hamill	Manchester United
1910	J. Walker	Bury
1912	W. Bookman	Bradford City
1912	F. McKee	Bradford City
1913	W. Lavery	Middlesborough
1913	W. Crone	Glasgow Celtic
1920	G. Barrett	Chelsea
1920	J. Ferris	Chelsea
1920	D. McKinney	Hull City
1920	M. Hamill	Manchester City
1920	J. Mulligan	Manchester City
1920	F. Carroll	Manchester City
1920	P. Kelly	Manchester City
1927	W. Scott	Lancaster Town
1932	G. Frewen	Wrexham
1933	A. Carroll	Clyde
1934	J. Coulter	Everton
1934	D. Martin	Wolves
1934	J. Brown	Wolves
1935	K. McCullough	Manchester City
1936	J. Feenan	Sunderland
1936	T. Breen	Manchester United
1938	J. McAlinden	Portsmouth
1947	J. Vernon	West Bromwich Albion
1947	E. McMorran	Manchester City
1948	C. Tully	Glasgow Celtic
1949	J. Campbell	Fulham
1949	R. Lawlor	Fulham
1949	T. Aherne	Luton
1949	P. Bonnar	Barnsley
1949	C. Currie	Bradford
1949	G. Haslett	Bury

Irish League Tables

Season 1896-97

	P	W	D	L	F	A	Pts
Glentoran	10	9	1	1	24	10	17
Cliftonville	10	4	3	3	22	20	11
Linfield	10	4	3	3	34	24	11
Distillery	10	3	3	4	17	23	9
North Staffordshire	10	2	4	4	17	23	8
Belfast Celtic	**10**	**1**	**2**	**7**	**11**	**25**	**4**

Season 1897-98

	P	W	D	L	F	A	Pts
Linfield	10	8	1	1	22	10	17
Cliftonville	10	6	1	3	23	17	13
Glentoran	10	6	1	3	31	12	13
Belfast Celtic	**10**	**3**	**1**	**6**	**15**	**19**	**7**
Distillery	10	2	1	7	13	28	5
North Staffordshire	10	2	1	7	13	31	5

Season 1898-99

	P	W	D	L	F	A	Pts
Distillery	10	7	1	2	23	17	15
Linfield	10	7	1	2	21	8	15
Cliftonville	10	6	0	4	19	12	12
Glentoran	10	6	0	4	17	12	12
Belfast Celtic	**10**	**2**	**2**	**6**	**15**	**25**	**6**
North Staff.	10	0	0	10	11	32	0

Season 1899-1900

	P	W	D	L	F	A	Pts
Belfast Celtic	**8**	**5**	**1**	**2**	**18**	**11**	**11**
Linfield	8	3	4	1	16	10	10
Cliftonville	8	3	3	2	16	16	9
Distillery	8	2	4	2	11	13	8
Glentoran	8	0	2	6	7	18	2

(Royal Scots withdrew after 7 matches; their record was declared null and void)

Season 1900-01

	P	W	D	L	F	A	Pts
Distillery	10	7	2	1	33	10	16
Glentoran	10	7	1	2	24	13	15
Belfast Celtic	**10**	**4**	**2**	**4**	**13**	**13**	**10**
Cliftonville	10	3	4	3	17	18	10
Linfield	10	3	2	5	10	12	8
Derry Celtic	10	0	1	9	12	43	1

Season 1901-02

	P	W	D	L	F	A	Pts
Linfield	14	12	0	2	38	10	24
Glentoran	14	10	1	3	39	19	21
Distillery	14	8	3	3	38	20	19
Cliftonville	14	7	2	5	24	14	16
Belfast Celtic	**14**	**4**	**4**	**6**	**22**	**24**	**12**
Derry Celtic	14	5	2	7	23	26	12
Ulster	14	2	3	9	22	44	7
St Columb's Court	14	0	1	13	13	62	1

Season 1902-03

	P	W	D	L	F	A	Pts
Distillery	14	9	2	3	34	20	20
Linfield	14	8	3	3	36	16	19
Glentoran	14	7	3	4	30	18	17
Belfast Celtic	**14**	**7**	**2**	**5**	**35**	**23**	**16**
Derry Celtic	14	4	4	6	27	31	12
Cliftonville	14	5	3	6	17	21	11
Bohemians	14	3	3	8	22	26	9
Ulster	14	3	0	11	13	51	6

Season 1903-04

	P	W	D	L	F	A	Pts
Linfield	14	12	2	0	47	9	26
Distillery	14	8	4	2	35	13	20
Glentoran	14	7	6	1	20	9	20
Belfast Celtic	**14**	**5**	**2**	**7**	**27**	**20**	**12**
Cliftonville	14	5	2	7	22	29	12
Bohemians	14	4	3	7	24	33	11
Derry Celtic	14	3	2	9	17	26	8
Scott. Borderers	14	1	1	12	11	64	3

Season 1904-05

	P	W	D	L	F	A	Pts
Glentoran*	14	9	3	2	22	12	21
Belfast Celtic*	**14**	**9**	**3**	**2**	**21**	**10**	**21**
Linfield	14	6	4	4	18	12	16
Distillery	14	6	3	5	16	11	15
Cliftonville	14	6	1	7	17	17	13
Shelbourne	14	5	3	6	15	17	13
Derry Celtic	14	1	5	8	12	31	6
Bohemians	14	2	2	10	15	26	6

*Glentoran won championship play-off.

Season 1905-06

	P	W	D	L	F	A	PTs
Cliftonville	14	7	5	2	19	8	19
Distillery	14	8	3	3	20	13	19
Linfield	14	7	3	4	21	14	17
Belfast Celtic	**14**	**6**	**3**	**5**	**20**	**18**	**15**
Bohemians	14	5	2	7	17	20	12
Shelbourne	14	5	2	7	16	18	12
Derry Celtic	14	4	3	7	13	22	11
Glentoran	14	2	3	9	13	26	7

Season 1906-07

	P	W	D	L	F	A	PTs
Linfield	14	10	3	1	30	9	23
Shelbourne	14	8	3	3	27	21	19
Distillery	14	6	4	4	27	22	16
Cliftonville	14	4	6	4	18	16	14
Bohemians	14	4	5	5	19	22	13
Belfast Celtic	**14**	**4**	**3**	**7**	**18**	**25**	**11**
Glentoran	14	2	5	7	18	25	9
Derry Celtic	14	2	3	9	11	28	7

Season 1907-08

	P	W	D	L	F	A	PTs
Linfield	14	10	2	2	31	15	22
Glentoran	14	7	3	4	27	23	17
Cliftonville	14	6	5	3	22	16	17
Distillery	14	6	2	6	21	21	14
Shelbourne	14	6	2	6	22	17	14
Belfast Celtic	**13**	**5**	**1**	**7**	**20**	**20**	**11**
Derry Celtic	14	4	1	9	16	30	9
Bohemians	13	2	2	9	13	30	6

Season 1908-09

	P	W	D	L	F	A	PTs
Linfield	14	10	1	3	27	13	21
Glentoran	14	8	3	3	29	22	19
Shelbourne	14	7	1	6	20	20	15
Distillery	14	6	1	7	22	19	13
Bohemians	13	6	1	6	28	29	13
Belfast Celtic	**14**	**5**	**2**	**7**	**26**	**33**	**12**
Cliftonville	13	4	2	7	17	19	10
Derry Celtic	14	4	0	10	12	26	8

Season 1909-10

	P	W	D	L	F	A	Pts
Cliftonville	14	8	4	2	25	14	20
Belfast Celtic	**14**	**9**	**0**	**5**	**25**	**13**	**18**
Linfield	14	5	5	4	19	20	15
Distillery	14	5	3	6	14	13	13
Derry Celtic	14	4	5	5	19	21	13
Bohemians	14	4	3	7	20	31	11
Glentoran	14	5	1	8	23	23	11
Shelbourne	14	2	7	5	15	24	11

Season 1910-11

	P	W	D	L	F	A	Pts
Linfield	14	9	4	1	29	11	22
Glentoran	14	10	2	2	39	12	22
Belfast Celtic	**14**	**5**	**5**	**4**	**21**	**19**	**15**
Cliftonville	14	5	4	5	16	22	14
Derry Celtic	14	5	4	5	21	29	14
Shelbourne	14	3	4	7	15	31	10
Distillery	14	2	5	7	13	19	9
Bohemians	14	1	4	9	14	25	6

Season 1911-12

	P	W	D	L	F	A	Pts
Glentoran	14	10	3	1	41	11	23
Distillery	14	9	3	2	32	14	21
Belfast Celtic	**14**	**7**	**6**	**1**	**21**	**11**	**20**
Linfield	14	6	4	4	25	16	16
Derry Celtic	14	5	1	8	16	30	11
Shelbourne	14	2	4	8	10	28	8
Cliftonville	14	3	1	10	14	36	7
Glenavon	14	2	2	10	17	30	6

Season 1912-13

	P	W	D	L	F	A	Pts
Glentoran	18	12	2	4	35	16	26
Distillery	18	11	2	5	34	17	24
Linfield	18	9	5	4	29	23	23
Glenavon	18	9	2	7	25	17	20
Cliftonville	18	8	3	7	23	23	19
Bohemians	18	8	2	8	31	29	18
Belfast Celtic	**18**	**7**	**4**	**7**	**24**	**26**	**18**
Shelbourne	18	7	4	7	20	23	18
Derry Celtic	18	3	3	12	18	39	9
Tritonville	18	2	1	15	27	55	5

Season 1913-14

Linfield	14	11	2	1	32	13	24
Glentoran	14	8	3	3	32	18	19
Belfast Celtic	**14**	**8**	**1**	**5**	**19**	**18**	**17**
Distillery	14	6	4	4	14	12	16
Shelbourne	14	6	2	6	16	10	14
Glenavon	14	4	2	8	12	23	10
Bohemians	14	2	2	10	19	36	6
Cliftonville	14	3	0	11	15	29	6

Season 1914-15

Belfast Celtic	**14**	**10**	**3**	**1**	**24**	**7**	**23**
Glentoran	14	9	3	2	27	11	21
Linfield	14	6	5	3	27	18	17
Distillery	14	7	1	6	23	16	15
Shelbourne	14	6	3	5	17	13	15
Glenavon	14	3	5	6	24	27	11
Cliftonville	14	4	1	9	14	29	9
Bohemians	14	0	1	13	10	45	1

During World War I no competitions held between 1915 and 1919

Season 1919-20

Belfast Celtic	**14**	**10**	**3**	**1**	**27**	**6**	**23**
Distilery	14	7	6	1	26	6	20
Glentoran	14	8	3	3	29	10	19
Linfield	14	4	4	6	8	11	12
Shelbourne	14	3	6	5	16	21	12
Glenavon	14	3	4	7	21	28	10
Cliftonville	14	2	5	7	9	15	9
Bohemians	14	2	2	10	5	37	7

Belfast Celtic didn't partake in the league between 1920 and 1924

Season 1924-25

Glentoran	22	17	3	2	53	18	37
Queens Island	22	13	6	3	48	23	32
Belfast Celtic	**22**	**11**	**5**	**6**	**36**	**31**	**27**
Portadown	22	10	5	7	41	35	25
Glenavon	22	11	2	9	45	36	24
Linfield	22	10	2	10	34	31	22
Ards	22	7	4	11	39	41	18
Larne	22	7	4	11	30	47	18
Barn United	22	6	4	12	29	40	16
Cliftonville	22	6	4	12	21	32	16
Distillery	22	6	4	12	31	40	16
Newry Town	22	5	3	14	34	67	13

Season 1925-26

Belfast Celtic	**22**	**16**	**1**	**5**	**52**	**38**	**33**
Glentoran	22	13	4	5	52	30	30
Larne	22	11	5	6	49	33	27
Ards	22	11	4	7	56	43	26
Distillery	22	10	5	7	37	35	25
Queen's Island	22	9	5	8	42	37	23
Glenavon	22	10	3	9	35	37	23
Linfield	22	8	5	9	47	50	21
Portadown	22	7	7	8	43	41	21
Newry Town	22	5	5	12	33	51	15
Cliftonville	22	4	6	12	29	37	
Bangor	22	2	2	18	25	64	6

Season 1926-27

Belfast Celtic	**22**	**15**	**7**	**0**	**66**	**26**	**37**
Queens Island	22	12	6	4	46	34	30
Distillery	22	12	5	5	56	36	29
Glentoran	22	11	5	6	56	47	27
Ards	22	9	7	6	42	42	25
Larne	22	10	4	8	55	48	24
Linfield	22	8	6	8	41	35	22
Portadown	22	7	4	11	50	48	18
Cliftonville	22	7	3	12	32	40	17
Newry Town	22	6	5	11	39	48	17
Glenavon	22	4	3	15	33	57	11
Barn United	22	2	3	17	35	89	7

Season 1927-28

Belfast Celtic	**26**	**20**	**5**	**1**	**101**	**35**	**45**
Linfield	26	18	5	3	88	34	41
Newry Town	26	13	7	6	55	30	33
Larne	26	13	4	9	63	55	30
Glentoran	26	12	5	9	63	65	29
Coleraine	26	11	5	10	57	60	27
Distillery	26	9	7	10	45	44	25
Bangor	26	9	5	12	57	69	23
Glenavon	26	9	5	12	63	69	23
Portadown	26	10	3	13	61	58	23
Ards	26	8	5	13	54	69	21
Queens Island	26	5	7	14	46	69	17
Barn United	26	5	4	17	38	91	14
Cliftonville	26	5	3	18	29	72	13

Season 1928-29

Belfast Celtic	26	22	4	0	116	23	48
Linfield	26	19	1	6	88	44	39
Glentoran	26	15	3	8	85	59	33
Distillery	26	15	2	9	71	58	32
Coleraine	26	13	4	9	63	53	30
Ballymena United	26	10	8	8	63	55	28
Bangor	26	10	6	10	49	52	26
Glenavon	26	8	8	10	61	63	24
Ards	26	9	5	12	55	64	23
Newry Town	26	9	4	13	46	58	22
Portadown	26	10	2	14	52	76	22
Larne	26	8	4	14	49	75	20
Cliftonville	26	3	4	19	32	73	10
Queens Island	26	2	3	21	53	130	7

Season 1929-30

Linfield	26	19	4	3	92	44	42
Glentoran	26	16	4	6	79	53	36
Coleraine	26	14	4	8	66	46	32
Belfast Celtic	26	13	4	9	68	57	30
Bangor	26	12	5	9	60	57	29
Ballymena United	26	13	3	10	65	46	29
Derry City	26	12	5	9	52	55	29
Distillery	26	12	3	11	65	62	27
Glenavone	26	12	3	11	70	63	27
Portadown	26	7	7	12	68	90	21
Newry Town	26	9	1	16	51	66	19
Ards	26	6	6	14	47	77	18
Larne	26	5	3	18	47	77	13
Cliftonville	26	5	2	19	40	77	12

Seasons 1930-31

Glentoran	26	22	3	1	96	39	47
Linfield	26	16	6	4	73	42	38
Belfast Celtic	26	16	4	6	75	52	36
Distillery	26	15	4	7	82	46	34
Ballymena United	26	13	5	8	75	51	31
Ards	26	11	5	10	68	69	27
Derry City	26	10	4	12	50	61	24
Cliftonville	26	11	2	13	54	70	24
Portadown	26	7	5	14	63	73	19
Bangor	26	7	5	14	62	75	19
Glenavon	26	8	3	15	47	76	19
Coleraine	26	6	6	14	48	56	18
Larne	26	6	6	14	44	73	18
Newry Town	26	4	2	20	54	100	10

Season 1931-32

Linfield	26	20	3	3	78	32	43
Derry City	26	16	6	4	61	30	38
Belfast Celtic	26	14	5	7	55	36	33
Coleraine	26	13	6	7	67	54	32
Glentoran	26	12	7	7	73	54	31
Clioftonville	26	11	5	10	59	55	27
Ballymena United	26	11	5	10	65	41	27
Distillery	26	8	7	11	57	68	23
Portadown	26	8	6	12	54	63	22
Newry Town	26	9	4	13	43	53	22
Larne	26	6	7	13	47	85	19
Ards	26	7	4	15	52	81	18
Glenavon	26	6	5	15	42	74	17
Bangor	26	3	6	17	41	68	12

Season 1932-3

Belfast Celtic	26	19	3	4	81	34	41
Distillery	26	18	3	5	75	47	39
Linfield	26	17	4	5	83	34	38
Derry City	26	16	1	9	59	39	33
Glentoran	26	14	4	8	74	61	32
Bangor	26	13	2	11	60	56	28
Coleraine	26	11	5	10	69	50	27
Ballymena United	26	11	4	11	56	58	26
Glenavon	26	7	4	15	56	59	18
Portadown	26	8	2	16	37	72	18
larne	26	8	1	17	55	88	17
Ards	26	6	5	15	51	83	17
Cliftonville	26	5	6	15	54	74	16
Newry Town	26	5	4	17	47	102	14

Season 1933-34

Linfield	26	22	2	2	88	21	46
Belfast Celtic	26	17	3	6	74	42	37
Glentoran	26	16	3	7	59	36	35
Distillery	26	14	3	9	61	41	31
Baallymena United	26	12	6	8	59	46	30
Ards	26	11	5	10	47	46	27
Portadown	26	10	5	11	41	52	25
Glenavon	26	10	4	12	45	54	24
Derry City	26	8	7	11	37	38	23
Cliftonville	26	11	0	15	50	78	22
Bangor	26	7	4	15	43	58	18
Coleraine	26	7	3	16	40	61	17
Newry Town	26	5	6	15	37	71	16
Larne	26	4	5	17	37	74	13

Season 1934-35

Linfield	26	21	4	1	76	19	46
Derry City	26	18	4	4	64	32	40
Belfast Celtic	**26**	**17**	**3**	**6**	**96**	**36**	**37**
Glentoran	26	16	4	6	70	42	36
Poeradown	26	14	5	7	56	38	33
Distillery	26	11	5	10	47	44	27
Larne	26	11	5	10	48	53	27
Glenavon	26	7	7	12	43	55	21
Ballymena United	26	7	5	14	48	65	19
Cliftonville	26	8	3	15	45	69	19
Newry Town	26	8	1	17	60	76	17
Coleraine	26	7	2	17	43	66	16
Ards	26	5	3	18	46	91	13
Bangor	26	3	7	16	39	95	13

Season 1935-36

Belfast Celtic	**26**	**20**	**3**	**3**	**67**	**23**	**43**
Derry City	26	18	5	3	71	36	41
Linfield	26	17	4	5	72	28	38
Newry Town	26	14	5	7	80	50	33
Glentoran	26	12	3	11	57	50	27
Distillery	26	11	5	10	50	52	27
Larne	26	11	4	11	49	65	26
Portadown	26	9	5	12	53	58	23
Cliftonville	26	9	5	12	49	61	23
Ballymena United	26	7	5	14	41	59	19
Bangor	26	8	3	15	47	72	19
Glenavon	26	6	5	15	40	56	17
Coleraine	26	5	5	16	28	44	15
Ards	26	5	3	18	44	94	13

Season 1936-37

Belfast Celtic	**26**	**20**	**4**	**2**	**86**	**21**	**44**
Derry City	26	20	3	3	84	36	43
Linfield	26	20	2	4	85	25	42
Portadown	26	14	4	8	49	38	32
Larne	26	13	2	11	63	57	28
Newry Town	26	12	3	11	59	48	27
Glentoran	26	11	3	12	65	65	25
Cliftonville	26	9	6	11	55	63	24
Glenavon	26	10	1	15	56	59	21
Bangor	26	8	3	15	40	80	19
Coleraine	26	7	5	14	25	60	19
Ards	26	8	2	16	42	73	18
Distillery	26	6	2	18	36	65	14
Ballymena United	26	3	2	21	33	88	8

Season 1937-38

Belfast Celtic*	**26**	**18**	**5**	**3**	**86**	**22**	**41**
Derry City*	26	20	1	5	81	40	41
Portadown	26	16	5	5	67	32	37
Linfield	26	16	5	5	78	38	37
Ballymena United	26	14	5	7	72	55	33
Glentoran	26	15	2	9	64	57	32
Newry Town	26	10	6	10	63	49	26
Distillery	26	10	6	10	51	61	26
Ards	26	7	4	15	43	66	18
Glenavon	26	6	5	15	36	55	17
Bangor	26	7	2	17	39	62	16
Larne	26	6	3	17	48	87	15
Coleraine	26	5	5	16	40	75	15
Cliftonville	26	2	6	18	27	86	10

*Belfast Celtic won championship play-off.

Season 1938-39

Belfast Celtic	**26**	**19**	**2**	**5**	**97**	**32**	**40**
Ballymena United	26	15	5	6	63	54	35
Derry City	26	15	3	8	84	46	33
Portadown	26	15	3	8	84	56	33
Linfield	26	14	2	10	58	40	30
Glentoran	26	14	1	11	64	68	29
Glenavon	26	12	4	10	67	57	28
Ards	26	11	6	9	63	66	28
newry Town	26	9	8	9	43	48	26
Distillery	26	9	4	13	53	56	22
Larne	26	8	4	14	45	74	20
Bangor	26	6	7	13	38	72	19
Cliftonville	26	5	2	19	38	81	12
Coleraine	26	3	3	20	40	87	9

Season 1939-40

Belfast Celtic	**26**	**20**	**5**	**1**	**91**	**18**	**45**
Portadown	26	18	5	3	86	37	41
Glentoran	26	19	1	6	103	45	39
Ballymena	26	15	4	7	82	52	34
Linfield	26	13	5	8	62	48	31
Derry City	26	14	2	10	73	46	30
Glenavon	26	13	3	10	69	68	29
Ards	26	11	2	13	52	69	24
Coleraine	26	10	2	14	45	70	22
Bangor	26	8	3	15	44	77	19
Distillery	26	6	3	17	53	70	15
Newry Town	26	5	5	16	32	86	15
Larne	26	4	5	17	36	83	13
Cliftonville	26	3	1	22	40	99	7

Season 1947-48

Belfast Celtic	**22**	**19**	**1**	**2**	**84**	**26**	**39**
Linfield	22	15	5	2	55	19	35
Ballymena United	22	10	7	5	52	38	27
Distillery	22	12	2	8	35	32	26
Glentoran	22	9	8	5	44	29	26
Coleraine	22	8	6	8	48	46	22
Glenavon	22	8	6	8	45	45	22
Ards	22	7	4	11	39	59	18
Cliftonville	22	7	4	11	36	47	18
Bangor	22	6	4	12	34	50	16
Portadown	22	3	3	16	31	60	9
Derry City	22	2	2	18	18	70	6

Season 1948-49

Linfield	22	16	4	2	58	21	36
Belfast Celtic	**22**	**14**	**3**	**5**	**69**	**32**	**31**
Glentoran	22	13	3	6	45	28	29
Cliftonville	22	9	5	8	44	38	23
Bangor	22	8	5	9	43	45	21
Distillery	22	9	3	10	51	56	21
Portadown	22	8	4	10	41	48	20
Glenavon	22	6	8	8	35	43	20
Derry City	22	8	3	11	39	58	19
Ballymena United	22	6	7	9	40	52	19
Ards	22	7	2	13	46	49	16
Coleraine	22	4	1	17	25	66	9

American Tour Results - 1949

May 8	(New York)	Celtic 2	New York All-Stars 2
May 12	(Toronto)	Celtic 5	Ulster United 0
May 14	(New Jersey)	Celtic 3	New Jersey Stars 0
May 18	(Falls River)	Celtic 1	New England All-Stars 2
May 25	(Philadelphia)	Celtic 6	Philadelphia All-Stars 4
May 29	(New York)	Celtic 2	Scotland 0
May 30	(New York)	Celtic 3	Philadelphia Nationals 3
June 1	(Montreal)	Celtic 4	Montreal All-Stars 1
June 5	(Detroit)	Celtic 4	Dave Kennedy F.C. 2
June 12	(New York)	Celtic 0	Kamraterna (Sweden) 3